THE HIDDEN CREATOR

BY
HILTON HOTEMA

978-1-63923-480-6

Printed: October 2022

Cover Art By: Amit Paul

Published and Distributed By:
Lushena Books
607 Country Club Drive, Unit E
Bensenville, IL 60106
www.lushenabks.com

ISBN: 978-1-63923-480-6

THE HIDDEN CREATOR

+

By

Prof. Hilton Hotema

(1961)

As Above, So below

The Creator Is Reflected In His Creations

The True Doctrine of Omnipresence means
the Creator appears in every moss and
every cobweb.
                        - Emerson.

Nowhere in this work are we directed to
do anything, nor are we condemned for what
we do. It is the office of higher intelligence to show humans how unwise words and
works harm them, and to warn them that they
will reap as they sow.
                        - Hotema.

PROLOGUE

The central current of the flood of religious works pouring forth from the press, flows in different directions, according to the particular doctrine which the writer desires to impress upon his readers.

One author may be interested in matters relating to the Bible, another may be interested in the Church or Christ, and still another may be interested in the Creator and His Creations.

The world wants to know who, what, and where is the Creator. Ages of searching by great men have failed to find Him. If there is a Creator, it should be possible to locate Him. If there is none, then there is no answer to the question, What Power Creates and Regulates the World and everything in it?

All questions have answers. This one has an answer, and Hotema was determined not to stop digging till he found it. Where did he find it? Right in the Bible, but stated in terms so simple that no one had noticed it.

Great scientists with giant telescopes peer outward in their effort to find the Outer Limits of the Universe. With powerful microscopes they search as diligently for the Origin of the Universe. A great game in either direction; very exciting, but yielding no satisfactory results.

Hotema took another course. He studied the Looker and discovered the Looker cannot see that which looks. The Looker can look only at some other object than itself. All the Looker can see has been created or it would not be present to be seen. All objects which can be seen, says the Bible, are temporal and have been created, and anything that cannot be seen is eternal and has not been created. The Looker cannot see itself, hence it has never been created.

A very valuable discovery. There is only one fundamental prerequisite to seeing anything _ it must be created and, hence, temporal. And by further analysis, it becomes certain that the Looker which is not seen has never been created, and therefore is eternal.

The Creator cannot be seen, and is, therefore, uncreated and eternal. He is the primary, absolute Reality, whose existence is revealed only by His work. In His work He is reflected, and appears in every plant and planet, in every moss and tree, in every bird and bee, in every mouse and man. That is the true doctrine of Omnipresence.

The Bible says, "The Kingdom of God is within you." Had the author or interpreter of that great passage operated on a level but one step higher in his understanding, the single word "within" had never been included; and so much different might have been the story of human history.

The clergy plod blindly on with mulish faith in creed and dogma, paral_ leling the scientist in peering forever outward in his search for the Kingdom of God within. Some day these converging lines of search may meet in the staggering light of KNOWINGNESS, thus ending the long dark night in which men walk and work.

Prof. Hilton Hotema: Born in Massachusetts February 7. 1878. This picture taken in Manila, Philippines. In April, 1901, after 16 months of battling with the Insurgents, participating in 39 engagements and skirmishes.

CREATION

In this Hunt For The Hidden Creator, we shall start our search by looking for the Door To The Hidden. And where would we reasonably expect to find that Door except right before our face in the form of Creation?

Nor must we allow ourself to be confused by the term Creation. If we go back to the Bible, a book that has been the authority on the subject of Creation for sixteen hundred years, we do not find anything helpful. It contains no scientific data of the Creation of the Universe. What it relates are traditional narratives based on ancient legends and fables. And furthermore, it presents three accounts, all of them different, each very brief, and none of any real value.

Why should the first of these biblical accounts end with the third verse of the second chapter of Genesis, while the second commences with the fourth verse of that same chapter, and relates a story that is entirely different from the first?

It appears from the clever arrangement that biblical compilers sought from the start to "create" confusion instead of order, to subvert the Mind instead of guiding it.

The second account extends thru the second and third chapters, coming to an end at the close of the fourth chapter. And then, in the fifth chapter, still another story begins, with this opening statement:

"This is the book (scroll) of the generations of Adam. In the day that God created man, in the likeness of God Made he him, male and female created he them, and called their name Adam, in the day when they were created."

This is evidently a man who is different from the one described in the first and second accounts. This first man was called Adam and had a wife named Eve, who bore two sons, named Cain and Abel. The later Adam mentioned in chapter five seems to have had no wife, being a perfect, biune, creative Unit; for of him the latter story says:

"Adam lived a hundred and thirty years, and begat a son in his own likeness, after his image (biune); and called his name Seth" (Gen. 5:3).

The author of this latest account appears to know nothing of Cain and Abel, the sons of Eve and the first Adam. They are mentioned in the second account, and then completely fade from the picture.

Some authorities notice this and assert that Cain and Abel were nothing more than symbols of the positive and negative poles of Creative Action. They hold that the same rule applies to Eve and the first Adam. These statements appear reasonable; for Polarity is the Great Law expressed by Creative Action; and the Bible is actually a book of symbolism, designed not to edify the exoteric but to lead astray the profane and the impious.

Dr. Kalisch, after referring to the first account of Creation in his Commentary on the Old Testament, wrote:

"Now the narrative seems not only to pause, but to go backward. The grand climax seems at once broken off, and the languid repetition appears to follow. Another cosmogony is introduced, which, to complete the perplexity, is, in many important features, in direct contradiction to the former" (p. 59).

The origin and the end of the world have been vital subjects of speculation since the dawn of human thought. The hypothesis of Creation by the fiat of a Creator, as presented in the first chapter of the Bible, failed to satisfy inquiring minds of deeper discernment.

Law, order, system, and process of development are so intimately related and conjoined, that the intelligent mind will not bring its searchings to an end, and rest its reason on the belief that a Creator, without the observance of law and order as revealed in Nature. by word of mouth and wave of hand, brought into existence, out of nothing, the varied forms and formations of the Universe.

Origen, the leading pupil of Flavius Titus Clement of Alexandria, and one of the best-informed and most learned of all the early Christian Fathers, said:

"If we hold to the letter (of the Bible) and must understand, after the manner of the common people, what stands written in the law, then I would blush with shame to confess aloud that it was God who has given these laws."

When Origen Considered the first book of the Bible, he observed: "What man of sense will agree with the (literal) statement (in the Bible) that the first, second and third days in which the Evening and the Morning are named, were without sun, moon and stars?

"What man is such an idiot as to suppose that God actually planted trees in Paradise, in Eden, like a husbandman? I believe that we must hold these statements (in the Bible) as images (allegories) under which a hidden meaning lies concealed."

We are approaching the Door To The Hidden Creator. But the public has never been told or taught, either by teacher or by pastor, that passages anywhere in the Bible are symbolical and allegorical; nor that these ancient fables cover and conceal from the eyes of the world certain remarkable and scientific facts concerning Creation and Creative Processes.

It is reasonable to assume that the early Christian Fathers who did the preliminary work in founding Christianity and in compiling the Bible, were far better informed than we as to the nature of the Ancient Scriptures and the hidden meaning of the Ancient Philosophy. What then,when such leading lights assert that certain passages in the Bible are images, symbols and allegories, "under which a hidden meaning lies concealed, " by what criterion are we to determine which passages in the Bible are to be construed literally and which symbolically?

In such a dilemma there is no logical alternative except to fall back on what we know of universal law, order, system, process of development and analogy, and base our considerations upon the premise that the only safe rule to guide us to the desired goal is what we know of Creation, Creative Processes, Universal Power and Universal Substance.

What is Creation? What started it? When and where did it begin? Whence the power, its nature, and the substance? How was the work done? Who directed and supervised the processes?

To these momentous questions the Bible furnishes no satisfactory answers, and for sixteen hundred years the Christian world had the use of no other ancient records to scan for the information.

The revelations of science gained in its researches of the last several centuries, indicate that Creation was not an original process which began, once upon a time, and then, at a later time,came to a sudden stop, as one is led to infer from the literal language of the

Bible, to the effect that "on the seventh day (of creation of the Universe) God ended his work which he had made" and took a rest (Gen. 2:3).

Science shows that there are no origins and no terminations. Creative Action is an endless cycle that had no beginning and can have no ending. It is a constant, perpetual process, a stream whose flow never began and whose end will never be.

This Endless Stream of Creative Action did not escape the attention of the Ancient Masters, and it was symbolized in Card No. 14 of their Tarot.

In that card is portrayed an Angel (Michael), archangel of Fire, standing with one foot on the land and the other on the sea. Behind him appears the Rising Sun of Creation, and above him the Rainbow, symbolizing the Septennial Qualities of Creation. His Pure White Robe signifies Creative Wisdom. At the neck thereof appears the Four Mystic Letters of the Tetragrammation, JHVH, representing the Ineffable Name and indicating the Four Great Elements of Creation, to the details of which we shall devote attention in due time. Below the letters is a Golden Star with Seven Points, symbolizing the Septennial Law of Creation, referred to frequently in the Bible, sometimes as Five Loaves and Two Fishes, Seven Angels with Trumpets, etc. (Mat. 14:17,19; Rev. 8:1-6).

In the Angel's hands are two cups, one of gold and one of silver, and flowing between them is the Endless Stream of Creation, symbolizing the Water of Life, the Life Essence of Creation, which sparkles with the Seven Colors of the Solar Spectrum. The cup in the one hand represents the past, the cup in the other hand represents the future, and the flowing stream between the cups represents the active present.

The Man of Darkness thinks that everything is incessantly flowing in one direction. The brainwashing, mind-conditioning processes of the schools are careful not to teach him anything about the Creative Cycle, in which everything constantly meets; that one thing comes from the past and the other from the future, and that Time is not a straight line, but a series of circles, turning in different directions

That is the inexorable course of Creative Action, known to the Ancient Masters ten thousand years ago, and recorded in their precious scrolls which were burned in the 4th, 5th, and 6th centuries A. D. We spend millions of dollars annually in our search for knowledge, and deliberately burn the Ancient Libraries to destroy Knowledge.

Continuity of existence is the only existence that can ever possibly be. Origins and terminations are states of fantasy, rising in the imagination from a lack of knowledge of Creation, and having acceptance only in blind belief.

Such imaginary states as eternal equilibrium, arrested action, motionless matter, the absolute of nothingness, either preceding origin or succeding termination, is positively unattainable in reality.

Not long ago, when modern science was clad in its swaddling-clout, and is still but little removed from that infantilic state, it posited space as definitely empty. Now it has suddenly reversed its primary postulate and flown off in the opposite direction, shouting with a loug voice as it flies, that everything known and unknown and unknown emerges from that former sea of nothingness.

Science is slyly embracing the ancient doctrine, but not admitting it, that the terrestrial world is a condensed formation of the Celestial Realm, mentioned in the Bible as the world called Heaven (2 Cor. 5:1). That the entire Universe is a huge mass of invisible Radiation, the visible portions thereof appearing as objects created of that Radiation; and that man, in his created body, lives and moves in that materialized image of the Celestial World of the Ancient Masters.

This is a Universe of Radiation, which the Ancient Masters called Astral Light. For want of a better term, science calls it Electricity. The radio telegraphic waves are manifestations of Electricity in motion.

Every existing object is recognized not so much from its particular form as from its electrical emanations, called its Auru. Electricity is better understood from its various phenomena than it is per se. All metals, rocks, vegetation, etc., are better known by their functions than by their physical formations.

Oxygen and hydrogen are invisible, odorless gases. Were it not for the fact that one supports combustion and the other does not, we could not differentiate these two gases. And so it is throughout the entire realm of the material world.

After more than a century of research and observation, science is beginning to grasp some of these fundamental facts of Creation.

-7-

It is beginning to realize that it was wrong in its former opinion, that the forces of the Universe were blind, non-intelligent, and operated without a definite purpose.

Listen to what the great Dr. Alexis Carrel said : "Everyone is aware that space is curved, that the world is composed of blind and unknown forces, that we are nothing but infinitely small particles on the surface of a grain of dust lost in the immensity of the cosmos, and that this cosmos is totally deprived of life and consciousness. Our universe is exclusively mechanical. It cannot be otherwise, since it has been created from an unknown substratum by the techniques of physics and astronomy" (Man The Unknown, p. 26).

Later, Carrel very inconsistently admits in his book that "The existence of intelligence is a primary datum of observation." He terms it a power and said, "This power of discerning the relations between things, assumes a certain value and a certain form in each individual. Intelligence is measurable by appropriate techniques. These measurements deal only with a conventional aspect of the mind. They do not give an accurate idea of intellectual value, but they permit a rough classification of human beings" (Man The Unknown, p. 121).

Let us briefly notice Creative Action and determine whether Intelligence of a primary datum of observation:

We plant a seed in the soil. In the course of time a tree comes forth. The seed attains a definite goal according to a preordained plan. That is not the accidental course of blind force. Supreme Intelligence is presented in every Creative Process, and science cannot duplicate the most simple ones by any means at its command.

The hen lays an egg---and what could look more lifeless and senseless than an egg? Yet, after a few weeks of brooding, a living creature comes forth from that apparently lifeless and senseless egg.

Here is positive evidence to indicate that in that egg a mysterious force was present, possessing intelligence which directed the Creative Process to a definite goal, transforming the watery substance of the egg into an organized formation of blood, flesh, muscles, bones, and nerves possessing the power to see, hear, smell, feel, and taste, --all the structures required and necessary to produce a living animal, and endow it with all the powers required for it to live in perfect harmony with its environment, and to look after its wants and needs.

- 8 -

This is an illustration of the operation of the operation of a power, directed by intelligence, which performs Creative Processes in accordance with a pre-ordained plan; and the facts of the accomplishment contradict and refute almost every word uttered by Carrel in the above-quoted statement.

The data here presented should be kept in mind; for in these simple processes of Creation there are presented all the mystery related to the production and formation of everything in the world, including Man, the Lord of the whole Earth, as the Bible says (Zech. 4:14).

Consider the most common product of all Creation, such as a simple blade of grass, as the great Inventor Thomas Edison once observed, and it is beyond the ability of any man, with all his scientific acumen, to duplicate it by any means at his disposal.

In this Universe of Radiation, the Earth on which we live sails like a ship on the ocean. The Earth floats in an electrical sea, called the Atmosphere, so dense at sea-level that it exerts a pressure of approximately 14.7 pounds per square inch. A man of average size supports with his body a pressure of 30,570 pounds--equal to a solid cube of lead four feet high--but he knows it not because his body is made to resist it.

This same electricity we see in bolts of lightning, so powerful that it splits giant trees and melts rock. When we examine the spot where this work occurs, we find no evidence of the force or its nature. We are told it is all due to "ionization"--the separation of positive and negative charges of air molecules, cloud particles, rain, snow, and dust.

The Sun's ionizing force is constantly bombarding the upper atmosphere, freeing electrons and causing auroral displays. Ions are groups of atoms that have lost or gained one or more electrons, and therefore carry either positive or negative charges of electricity.

Ions are produced by the impact of cosmic radiation, and the Sun's ultra-violet rays contacting the atmosphere. The electrons knocked off, soon attach themselves to air molecules and dust particles.

Every speck of substance in the Universe is constituted of electricity, and if the reader will remember this it will make it easier for him to follow us later on. For as all substance is of an electrical nature, so all bodies and objects are constituted of that electrified material.

In every creative action, a force presenting dual powers is engaged, a positive and a negative power. The entire Universe, now declares science, is moved by the positive and negative powers of electrical action. All creative operations in the Universe, in its elements, and in its created formations, are the result of and are carried on by the same force.

Dr. Calicchio said, "Whether it be crystallizations or petrifactions, the growth of vegetation or its decomposition, motions and changes of air and water, or the crumbling particles of mountain rock, all the motions, visible and invisible, that occur in the mineral, vegetable, animal and humanal kingdoms, and in all their multifarious operations, are produced by electricity, which is the cosmic power that maintains the harmony and order of the Universe."

This declaration naturally raises the question, What of that vital energy exhibited by the living body which science asserts is produced by food? In his answer to that question the great Carrel shouted:

"The illusions of the mechanicists of the nineteenth century, the dogmas of Jacques Loeb, the childish physico-chemical conceptions of the human being, in which so many physiologists and physicians still believe, have to be definitely abandoned"--because recent discoveries prove they are grossly erroneous (Man The Unknown).

Carrel was shooting at the theory of Life contained in all medical works, and regularly taught in the schools and colleges, to the effect that "Life," as the renowned Dr. Wm. Osler claimed, "is the expression of a series of chemical changes" (Mod. Med. p. 39).

And there is all that the modern medical doctor knows about Life, about the functions of the body, and why it functions at all. When he treats the sick, he knows not what he's doing. He employs poisons called "medicine, in an effort to change the body's function, in accordance with the teachings of his school, not knowing of course what he is doing, for he cannot know when he knows nothing about the reason why the body functions.

The Universe, in all its various operations, manifests a silent but constant creativeness. It is necessary to strain the mind to its utmost limit to form a comprehensive understanding of these processes; and even so, it becomes apparent that the countless changes which occur, most of them being beyond the reach of eye or microscope, are so varied that only a small portion of them can ever come under direct observation. That is the reason why the invisible secrets of Creation

are so baffling. Yet, it is not necessary to know the whole in order
at least to appreciate the behavior of a part.

The physical eye can see substance in a state of compounds and
admixtures; but beyond that visible limit there exists a vast Universe
of such grandeur and mystery, with such imposing greatness and sub-
limity, that only a very small portion of it is unfolded to the human
mind, and its magnitude, its processes, its harmony, its order and
its system must convince the most obstinate to believe that there is
and must be some Supreme Creative Power.

The most significant and momentous discovery of science that has
solved many mysteries, is the fact that everything known is constituted of electricity, which, as stated, appears in two forms, (1) radiation and (2) concentration.

Creation, in all its processes and operations, functions in a
perfect, harmonious, co-ordinated manner, always in a forward, definite purposeful, orderly, systematic direction, in the utmost perfect precision, to a pre-ordained goal, from the making of a blade
of grass to the creation of a world, showing that a vast Fountain of
Power, free from adulteration and unvitiated, must exist in the
Universe.

This Cosmic Fountain of Power, possessing capabilities and capa-
cities to create, produce, mold and perform according to cosmic
patterns, the most stupendous illustration of which is the creation
of this perfect, faultless, invisible Universe, which modern science
is just dimly beginning to discover, as it peers into its magnificent, majestic, perfect architecture.

Science has also discovered that there is a strange law of
sameness that binds together the diverse elements of substance. Lakhovsky asserted that the whole Universe is knit together by a "plexus
of Cosmic Rays," and all forms of substance, ranging from rarefied
gas to petrified flesh, are simply varying degrees of condensation
of this plexus.

And so, the more we learn the more we discover that we live in a
world of illusion. The greatest illusion perhaps is that which con-
strains us to regard physical objects, including the human body, as
something separate and apart from Cosmic Radiation.

Follow us closely and learn with surprise that in Astral Rays,
Astral Light, everything lives, and moves, and has its being.

Chapter No. 2

SCIENTOLOGY

We live in a Christian World and our world is dominated completely by the dogmatisms of a physical science and a Christian theology. As science at this time is the primary ruler of our educational systems, it is in order to consider first the foundation of this science and the super-structure of its system, so that we may determine by the known facts of Creation whether this science is based upon factualities of fallacies.

It is well to understand at the start that this science sets on a foundation of materialism, and its superstructure is merely an extension thereof. Some of its fallacies we briefly noticed in the preceding chapter, and more are coming up for consideration and disposition.

After first assuming that everything in the Universe has a physical basis, this science sets out to determine the physical causes of its "psychical" facts. So long as it seeks only to relate physical causes with physical effects, it is admirable. But when it attempts to relate psychical phenomena with physical causes, it ignominiously fails.

The best intelligence of this day and time accepts most of the physical facts of Creation as collated and classified by physical science. But this same intelligence declines to accept the postulates advanced by physical science as to the causes of psychical phenomena.

These hypothetical dogmas, founded upon only some of the facts of Creation, bewildered even so great an intelligence as Thomas H. Huxley. Having accepted the physical facts of Darwinism, he felt bound to accept Darwin's speculations as to the causes of those facts.

As a result, Huxley repudiated Creation and denounced it as a monster without a single principle that presented either purpose or justice. He forced his reason to accept what his intuitions always denied, viz., that all we have, all we are, and all we may become, are merely the automatic results of breeding, feeding, and battling. It is not surprising that this great scientists declared Life to be an unsolvable riddle, intelligence a delusion, and love essentially lust.

The development of science is really a development of the Mind. The history of science is a history of the mental development of the scientist.

The indelible facts of history indicate that the only science of Creatology, Anthropology and Biology which the world has ever had, was the Cosmic Science developed by the Atlantean Astrologers over a period of many thousands of years, and then fanatically destroyed by the ignorant Roman Emperors as we have related elsewhere.

There exist today two systems of thought regarding Creation. One of these passes for current science and the other is regarded as superstition. We shall show in this discussion that the terms should be reversed.

Modern science asserts that it is impossible to get more energy out of a mechanism than is put into it, and then repudiates its own contention by conceiving of a Universe emerging out of nothingness. It holds that the mysterious qualities of Man, such as vitality, consciousness, mind and intelligence, just happen to rise out of matter, with no directing principle or controlling law, and that the mysterious process called Death means the total extinction and complete annihilation of living organisms and all of their qualities.

The other system, regarded by physical science as gross superstition, is founded upon the philosophy of the Ancient Wisdom, to the effect that human sight is deceptive and does not correspond to reality. We do not see what we think we see. More often, reality is the reverse of what we observe. For instance, instead of Death being the extinction of Man as claimed by physical science, it is a Creative Process of Transition to another state, and that is what we shall show is this discussion, and do it in such a convincing manner as to satisfy every one who is competent to think and reason.

These two systems of thought lead in opposite directions. The one goes inward and backward and is called the Inductive Process. The other goes outward and forward and is called the Deductive Process.

Sir Francis Bacon (1561-1626) and Auguste Comte (1798-1857) did the preliminary work that led to the founding of the Inductive System which in time became modern physical science. It is strictly a system of materialism.

These two men were constrained to take the course they did be-

-13-

cause they could not swallow the supernaturalism of theology, nor its terrible God of wrath, vengeance and murder, who countenanced and commanded the slaughter of men, women, children, and suckling infants (1 Sam. 15:2,3; Ezek. 9:5-7).

Let us quote from the Bible: "Thus sayeth the Lord God...slay every man his brother, and every man his companion, and every man his neighbor" (Exo⁻. 32:27). "The fathers shall eat the sons in the midst of thee, and the son shall eat their fathers" (Ezek. 5:10). "And I (God) will cause them to eat the flesh of their sons and the flesh of their daughters" (Jer. 19:9). "And ye shall eat the flesh of your sons, and the flesh of your daughters, shall ye eat" (Deut. 28:53-57; Lev. 26:25; Jer. 19:9; Lam. 4:10; 2 Kings 6: 28, 29).

As between a tyrannical God of murder, slaughter and cannibalism and no God at all, they opined that the world would be far better off without any God.

And that is the reason why these men chose what they considered the lesser of two evils. Having chosen their course, they were determined to leave no stone unturned, nor to refrain from any tricks in terminology or distortion of facts, to support their case and show the world that it was fallacious and fraudulent to contend that there was a God who would create Man for the purpose, or the pleasure, of murdering him and committing him to eternal torment, as taught by theology and bibliology, and then ask and expect this slave of a tyrant to worship that tyrant on his throne in his heavenly home.

So well did they accomplish their purpose, so strong was their determination to do the job, and so effective were their arguments to make their case "hold water," that the momentum of their chariot carried them and their followers so far in the opposite direction, that they got lost in the darkness which their work had created. And they are now slyly engaged in working their way out to the light. To hide their errors, they are using the most fraudulent tactics that the human mind can devise, as they seek to salvage some of the wreckage of their ship which occurred when the splitting of the atom exploded their bark.

It was the work of these determined warriors, who began back in that mental darkness of the Dark Ages when little was known about Creation and Creative Action, that profoundly influenced such noted men as Littre, Mill, Humboldt, Lewes, Grote, Darwin, Spencer, Wallace, Harrison, Huxley, Fiske, and a host of other protogonists of Evolution.

Their work laid the foundation of modern physical science, whose dogmas and hypotheses dominate our schools and colleges unto this day. Upon that same precarious foundation sets medical art, concerning which we shall have more to say in another place. And most of the uncertainty and confusion that exists in the world of science at this time, and in the realm of medical art, rises from the popular fallacies which have no basis in fact.

In the Inductive System we observe a number of fleeting facts, and on the grounds of analogy, extend what we think is true of these facts to other facts of the same category, thus arriving, as we think, at general principles or laws, and then the existence thereof we deny in our reasoning, which course is forced upon us to make the conclusion correspond with the premise.

The basic error here flows from the faulty conception of things and conditions that are regular in a constantly changing world, where we seldom see what we think we see. For these reasons, the observations and conclusions of the Inductionist are certain to be erroneous.

An excellent example to the point appears in the case of Christian Science. In 1875 Mary Baker Eddy published her remarkable book on the Science of Health, in which she made the then astounding assertion that Matter per se does not exist.

"For her daring to oppose a well-authenticated scientific dogma," -wrote H. G. Steele,"she was scouraged by members of the Modern Science Guild, one of whom quipped her assertion with the statement that her doctrine might be 'Christian,' but it most certainly was not 'Science.' Yet today, Matter, the beloved fetish of modern science, has been made to disappear completely behind the volubility of its own words. Did any one of them even nod his approval of the woman who pointed the way to their conclusions? To have done so would be to have understood the word 'humility.' And this word is not in the catechism of arrogant modern science."

In the Deductive System, the Wise Men of the Ancient World were searching for the facts of Creation, and were not ruled by commercialism. They based their work on a stable point, a General Principle of the Universe, and, on the basis of analogy, connected the known facts of Creation with individual cases by means of a chain of objects, all intimately related, leaving no interruptions to continuity. By this skilful process they consistently reduced the Universal to the Individual, affirming of the latter all of the distinctive qualities of the former.

The Masters opinionated that the great drama of Creation was enacted in the Starry Sky aeons and aeons before the earth was ever born. This formed the Starry Gospel of the Masters which imparts to him who can read the signs and symbols, a knowledge of his mystic being, and reveals the basic knowledge of the secret of Creation.

Then the Ancient Masters, to illustrate the essence of their discoveries and deductions, said, "As above, so below." As the Maker, so the Made. For Man upon the earth is created in the image and likeness of the Creator. It could not possibly be otherwise.

The Masters did not stop there. They went on to show why their deductions were sound and logical by declaring:

"The invisible things from the creation of the world are clearly seen (mentally), being known (and understood) by the things which are made" (visible) (Rom. 1:20).

And again: "We look not at the (created) things which are seen, but at the (uncreated) things which are not seen; for the (created) things which are seen are temporal (and illusional); but the (uncreated) things which are not seen are eternal" (and immortal) (2 Cor. 4:18).

At these solid, rock-bottom statements physical science sneeringly shouts, "Nothing but the empty utterances of superstitious heathens.

And these Inductionists have the brass to declare that their way is the only way of obtaining reliable knowledge. It has come to pass, under the pressure of physical science, that no system of endeavor is of any value except the Inductive. The actual facts are, nothing could be more unreliable, misleading, confusing and deceiving than a system of thought based upon the shaky evidence acquired by observation.

Physical science has extended its unreliable Inductive System to the processes of Creation, to created phenomena, and even to the human body, its conditions and functions, --thus making medical art nothing more than a faulty system of observation, assumption and speculation, with the brainwashed medics stupidly claiming that vaccination and inoculation will nulligy the Universal Law of Cuase and Effect, to the extent that man will not reap as he sows (Gal. 6:7).

The Inductive System consists of a ponderous mass of observed facts, organized it is true, but still a faulty mass in a faulty manner and, worst of all, minus and devoid of the Great Central Factor

which would explain all and correct all the confusion if it were discovered, recognized. and included in its proper place.

That Great Central Factor is the mysterious Unknowable Reality
which science claims, in one breath, is only a delusion and then
admits in the next breath that it does exist. but is so inconsequential and unrecognizable, and, therefore, not important.

Every way we turn, we find ourselves passing and repassing these
bewildered and confused Inductionists, who are trying this way then
that way in the hope of reaching the goal of their ambition.

Medical art is wasting millions of dollars of the public tax-
money and years of time in an effort to find ways and means to cir-
cumvent the Law of Cause and Effect, so man will not reap as he sows.
It points backward with pride through twenty-three centuries of blundering and confusion to Hippocrates as its patron saint, and in all
these centuries it has not uncovered even one specific "cure" for
"disease." Nor will there ever be any discovered for the simple
reason that disease, per se, does not exist except in the imagination of the medic.

It is their hopeless plight and the confused condition of their
minds which constrained us to be wiser and choose the forward and
outward course, the Deductive System of the Ancient Masters, and thus
pursue the scientific path which they travelled ten thousand years
ago, and leaving us an heritage so valuable that we have used it as
the foundation of our civilization.

As they did, so we follow them and start our work with a self-
existing General Principle, the Great Central Factor, the Mysterious
Power that does the work. And by logical steps and consistent pro-
cedure, we bring that Principle down to our level of understanding,
and apply it to the processes and the products of Creative Action,
leaving no loop holes to be plugged and no gaps to be bridged.

In a word, the success of our efforts depends upon the moving
of the Macrocosm down to the level of the Microcosm, expounding their
connection and relation, and affirming of the latter all the distinc-
tive qualities of the former, and vice versa.

We shall show in comprehensive terms what the Ancient Masters
meant when they wrote:

God created man in his own image and likeness.

The Kingdom of God is within you.

For in him we live, and move, and have our being.

Know we not that ye are the Temple of God, and that the Spirit of God dwelleth in you? If any man defile the Temple of God, him shall God destroy; for the Temple of God is holy, which Temple you are (1 Cor. 3:16).

What? Know ye not that your body is the Temple of the Holy Ghost which is in you, which ye have of God, and ye are not your own? For ye are bought with a price: therefore glorify God in your body, and in your spirit, which are God's (1 Cor. 5:19, 20)

When the Ancient Masters made these statements, they were engaged in serious work and were not peddling childish twaddle.

Chapter No. 3

OBSERVATION

We have spent some space and time in discussing the two great
systems of thought which prevail in the Christian World. We are at
a vital point that must not be passed too hastily, for we have corner-
ed here the profound mystery of Creation that has puzzled the best
brains in the Christian World for sixteen hundred years.

We especially indicate the Christian World because that is the
world which lost the Ancient Wisdom regarding Creation when it went
up in smoke as the arrogant Roman Emperors scornfully decreed the
burning of the ancient libraries, in order to annihilate the stupid
philosophy of the Ancient Heathens.

That wanton work of destruction of the Ancient Wisdom was carried out with such remarkable care, that Archbishop Chrysostom, in
the 5th Century A.D., declared; "Every trace of the old philosophy
and literature of the ancient world has vanished from the face of the
earth."

That declaration was practically true for more than fourteen
hundred years of darkness. But anything that has ever been can never
be completely eradicated and destroyed.

Light began to dawn in the darkness rather unexpectedly in 1799.
when Napoleon's army. while digging trenches in Egypt, chanced to
strick the now famous Rosetta Stone in the soil of the Nile delta,
where it had been deeply buried in the 4th Century by Constantine's
army of demolition.

Then there followed the marvellous work of Champollion in de-
ciphering the stone's crytic hieroglyphics. The result amazed the
Christian World; for that decipherment released the Ancient Voice of
the Superstitious Heathens which the Roman Emperors had tried to
silence forever.

The message on the stone revealed that it had been prepared in
195 B.C in honor of Ptolemy Epiphanes, and the inscription was dupli-
cated in three languages, --in Greek, in hieroglyphics, or sacred,

and in Demotic or common characters. It was this fact which enables Champollion, in 1822, to decipher it in the three languages, and thus recover the key for the reading of the ancient hieroglyphics, carved on the stone monuments and temples of Egypt, "the land of the Winged Globe," says the Masonic Encyclopedia, "the land of science and philosophy, peerless for stately tombs and magnificent temples, the land whose civilization was old and mature before other nations, later called to empires, even had a name."

We could not now be engaged in the preparation of this work, had it not been for the recovery of the message of the Ancient Voice of the Superstitious Heathens. That Voice, which the Roman Despots tried so hard to silence forever, now speaks to us again from the dim and distant past, with all its mighty power and proficiency, expounding that which we want to know most about the mystery of Creation. It all becomes more clear and comprehensive when the message of the Ancient Voice is added to the discoveries of Deductive Science.

We have said that modern science is the Inductive System. It dominates our educational systems, our schools, colleges, and medical institutions. It is based upon assumptions, speculations and postulations that have developed thru the years from the various observable EFFECTS that rise from the action of an unseen Power, called the Unknown Reality, the basic Cause of Existence and of all Effects.

While physical science is founded exclusively upon these illusional Effects, the Deductive System brushes these Effects aside as unreliable and delusional, and reasons from an Invisible Unity at the Center to a variety of Effects at the Visible Surface, thus following the regular order of all Creative Action, without an exception in the Universe, and the existence of Unity of Power at the center is indirectly admitted by the Inductionists by calling it the Unknowable Reality and referring to it as the Great First Cause. And then they conveniently disregard this basic Element, by passing it as Unknowable, Unrecognizable, Inconsequential, Inconspicuous and, therefore, Unimportant.

According to Inductive Science, Creation is "the integration of Matter and the concomitant dissipation of Motion," in harmony with the postulate that "all is physical matter and mechanical energy."

And so, the great element called Life is nothing more than a "Mode of Motion." In other words, Life is just the Effect of Motion. What is the Cause of the "motion"? What is the nature of the Power

that produces the "motion"? That is the Unknowable Reality, yet so
unimportant that it is pushed aside and omitted from any further
consideration by physical science.

Inductive Science reasons exclusively from OBSERVATION. That
is an unnatural and deceptional process, for--

> He saw with his own eyes the Moon is round;
> Was equally sure the Earth was square,
> As he'd travelled fifty miles, and found
> No sign that it was circular anywhere.
>
> ---Robert Walter.

As this is the deceptive premise from which physical science
reasons, its conclusions cannot be more reliable than the premise.
For every conclusion is an evolution of its postulated premise just
as certainly as every plant is an evolution of its seed.

As everything we know of the world around us is acquired thru
the limited and delusive sense powers, think how unreliable our normal conceptions are of the world in which we live.

Our physical eyes can see only the light band which is known as
the light spectrum, that range of color we see in the Rainbow, with
the color red at one edge and violet at the other.

This light spectrum comprises a very narrow band in the total
gamut of electro-magnetic radiation, with radio waves at the low
frequency end and x-rays, gamma rays and astral rays at the other
end.

At the lower end of the visible band there are infra-red and
heat, and above the visible band there are ultra-violet and a range
of experimental frequencies.

If we take a tape measure 300 yards long as representing the
total gamut, our physical eyes see only a little less than one inch.
All the rest is unseen and unknown to us.

Our ears are similarly limited in range. Sound is an aerial
vibration of frequencies between 16 waves per second and about 12,000
waves per second. Supersonic and ultrasonic sounds extend a long
way above this band, but are inaudible to our physical ears.

The other remaining senses are also very restricted in scope;
and on the basis of this limited knowledge gained by observation, we

dare to form fixed conceptions about the world and the things around us.

This means, among other things, that what we can see and hear comprises a very small fraction of what we could see and hear if our eyes and ears were capable of covering a wider portion of the total radiation gamut.

Recent experiments in extra-sensory perception prove that most of us possess latent power to extend the range of our normal senses and even, sometimes, add an additional sense such as telepathy. Clairvoyance and clairaudience are simply the extension of the normal range of our regular powers of seeing and hearing.

This brief consideration of the limited power and scope of our normal senses, as expounded by our accepted science, serves to shake our popular materialistic conceptions of Reality.

Due to the influences associated with the materialism of this age, modern man in the western world has lost conscious knowledge of his true nature and origin, his individualized overself, or true self as a unit of the one Life.

Deductive Science, on the other hand, is an unfolding of basic facts, corresponding to Creative Processes, as the bloom of the plant is an unfolding of its bud.

Creation in all instances, whether of a universe, a world, a living thing, a man, or a reliable system of thought, is an evolution, an unfolding of an Invisible Potency which, being positively existent contains within itself the promise and product of all that follows as the Effect.

And so, Deductive Reasoning proceeds from the Cause to the Effect, from the seed to the fruit, from the Principle to the Product, from the Creator to the Created, corresponding in all phases to all Creative Action. That system of reasoning reduces the complexities of Creed Phenomena to the simplicities of a stable system of science.

One of the most difficult problems is to form the realization the Creation is a stable system of order and harmony, resulting from the basic principle of Unity in Variety.

All that man observes in Creation, and all that he conceives in Thought, emanate from a Central Unity and is governed by one Law.

The Law is One, the Source is One, the Power is One, the Substance is One, and from this One there proceeds variety, each variety
a world in itself, impelled into motion by the internal Unknowable
Reality.

Emerson realized that all Existence is the result of a Central
Unity. In the Divinity College Address he said:

"The world is not the product of manifold powers, but of One
Will, of One Mind; and that One Mind is everywhere active, in each
Ray of the Star, and in each Wavelet of the Pool....The perception
of this Law of Laws awakens in the Mind of Man a sentiment which we
call the Religious Sentiment, and which makes our highest happiness
(when intelligently pursued).

"The Universe is represented in every one of its Particles.....
The World globes itself in the dew drop.....The True Doctrine of
Omnipresence is that the Creator appears with all His parts in every
moss and cobweb."

Not only is all Creation the product of one Force and governed
by one Law, but in the relationship of all parts and particles. The
result of this Principle of Unity in Variety is an ascending scale
of related phenomena in Creation, from the lowest to the highest forms,
from the mineral to the human.

Emerson declared: "It is a doctrine of philosophy that Man is
a being of degrees; that there is nothing in the world which is not
repeated in his body, his body being a sort of Miniature or Summary
of the World. Then there is nothing in his body which is not repeated
as in a Celestial Sphere of his Mind."

Creation, in all the variety of its forms, appears to the Human
Mind as a Mass of Symbols that represent Reality in the Whole and in
every Part. Each particular body is analogous to the whole, yet it
possesses its own Individuality.

The products of Creation are multifarious, even beyond human
comprehension, but Causes, on the contrary, are few in number, simple
in character, and certain in action.

Having discovered the Cause of any class of Effects, we attain
to a certainty of knowledge which is definite, and contrasts gloriously with the confused speculations of Inductive, Modern Science.

All principles are causes, all causes are forces, and all forces
operate in a fixed, changeless manner, which reveals the law of operation.

-23-

To reduce the complexities of Creation to the simplicities of science, requires, primarily, a discovery of the Law of Action,which, sustained by its corresponding phase of force, produces, controls, and explains all created phenomena of its class.

When we have discovered the Law which appears in the fixed, orderly operation of all Creative Action, we can formulate a definite Science of Creation. That is the point toward which we are proceeding, and when we unfold and present the result of our reasoning, he who can think will see how fallacious and erroneous are the findings and conclusions of modern science as to the quality, character, cause and source of the mysterious element called Life, and the equally mysterious process called Death.

Chapter No. 4

EVOLUTION

With the loss of the Ancient Wisdom, all of Europe and the
Roman Empire sank into mental darkness that lasted for a thousand
years. and even the rulers of kingdoms could neither read nor write.

There was no knowledge of Creation, of Life, of Man beyond the
pages of the Bible, and during those dark ages the Bible was not
available to the common people.

In referring to these things, Prof. Roswell D. Hitchcock, D.D.,
LL.D., in his analysis of the Bible, stated that, during this dark
period of time, the "reading of the Bible was prohibited by both
church and state" (p. 1159).

That was the approximate condition of knowledge in the Christian
World when the 19th Century dawned, and with that dawning there
developed a movement which caused the Christian World grave concern.

In referring to that 19th Century as "The Wonderful Century,"
John H. Deitrich showed in his book that it was in that century when
the "Fathers of Evolution" appeared. They set out to solve the mystery of Man, and he lists the leading ones as Darwin, Wallace,Spencer,
Fiske, Huxley and Haeckel, and added:

"There is no group of men in all history for which I have
greater admiration."....."No group of men ever worked together in
greater harmony or with more mutual consideration and affection than
this noble band of Pioneers in a great cause" (Fathers of Evolution,
p. 10).

When Charles Darwin's "Origin of Species" was published in 1859,
called by Marshall J. Gauvin, "a book that established the Doctrine
of Evolution upon a scientific foundation," the Christian World was
shocked, and its wrath fell upon Darwin's back. But physical science
was filled with joy, for at last the mystery of Man had been solved.

C. A. Wall, M.D., Ph. G., Ph.M., wrote a book of 600 pages, published in 1922, in which we said:

-25-

"I graduated as a physician from Bellevue Medical College in the same year that Darwin published his work on the Descent of Man. The 'Conflict between Science and Religion' which ensued, was fought out, and the truth of the theory of evolution was established within the period of my professional career. And with this victory of human thought, many superstitions faded away" (p.37).

And so, the physicians and surgeons graduate from medical institutions and take over their part of the world's affairs, thoroughly steeped in the postulate that Man is an improved Ape, and the great element called Life is nothing more than a "Mode of Motion."

And be it known that the "American Medical Association, the most powerful labor union in existence, has succeeded in entrenching itself and its stupid doctrines behind a mass of legislative enactments unparallelled by even the church at its worst. And so completely 'scientific' is this vaunted system, which points backward with pride through twenty-three hundred years of blundering and confusion to Hippocrates as its patron saint, that in all these centuries it has not uncovered even one specific cure for disease," wrote H. G. Steele.

Prof. Henry Drummond was highly elated over the theory of Evolution that swept the world of physical science in the 19th century. He was certain that the mystery of Man had been solved, and discussed the subject with great fluence in his book, "Natural Law In The Spiritual World," published in 1883, but even more fully in his "Ascent of Man," concluding the latter with a chapter of Involution, in which he reiterated the arguments of his Natural law, and urged that the "Supreme factor in all development is Environment....Every living thing lives in correspondence with its Environment." He said:

"Tree and root find their explanation not in something in themselves, but mainly in something outside of themselves. The secret of Evolution lies, in short, with Environment."

Then, in an attempt to make his speculations more solid, he declared:

"Evolution is not to unfold from within; it is to infold from without" (Ascent of Man, p. 324).

Prejudiced men, not searching for facts, invent their terminology and define their terms to fit their theories.

It is amazing how blind that prejudice can made a man, and how closely men can cut to the line, and yet miss the vital point because of their prejudical blindness.

Tree and root do absolutely find their explanation within
themselves. That is the very condition of their existence. That
condition is the internal power which gives them the ability to adjust themselves to the state of their environment. Ctherwise they
would perish. The power of adjustment abides within the organism,
and is called into action when necessary to save Life by adjusting
the body to its environment.

Environment does not produce living organisms, but it exercises
a powerful influence upon them. Col. Churchward told us in chapter
7 of this, his work,that the Condition of the Environment is the
Parent of the Creation.

Living organisms are adaptations, and when their condition fails
to harmonize with the condition of the environment, they begin to
degenerate and go to an early grave.

That is the scientific explanation of the reason for the disap-
pearance of the gigantic beasts of prehistoric times, when their
environment changed to the extent that the bodies of these beasts
had not the adapted changes to meet the change, they perished.

To cover this subject adequately would require a big book. It
would explain why the new-born infant soon develops a cold and mucus
begins to flow from its nose. That is the deadly work of polluted
air; and vital statistics show that the majority of children who die
under the age of ten years, are killed by disorders of the air organs.
After that age, the vital powers of the body have had time to adjust
the organism to the polluted air of its environment, and disorders
of the air organs decrease. But that does not stop the degenerative
work of the polluted air. It only changes the type of the body's
derangement, which soon appear in the form of some chronic disorder.

The baisc question here is, are vital phenomena the product of
environment or of internal Power? Is the Life of the living organism
dependent upon food, as medical art so strongly contends, or does it
simply use the food for its purposes?

If Life depends upon food, then man should never die as long as
he can eat and has an ample food supply. But the facts of daily observation and experience prove that food does not sustain Life in the
body. Then why do we eat? That is another big question and we have
discussed it at length in another work.

In the 19th Century a group of eminent doctors in Europe   made
a long investigation of the relationship between food and the living

organism.

Their findings constrained them to issue a surprising statement.
They said "We eat to live, and we eat to die."

That caused us to make a deep study of the whole subject, and
our findings amazed us. They were publised in 1952 and should be
read by every man.

Herbert Spencer, the great evolutionist, devoted many chapters
of his writings to the elucidation of theories upon which to base
a definition of Life. He missed the point because he did not begin
at the beginning. Like the pure Evolutionist, he presumed the existence of living matter to start with, without explaining where he
got it, or what made it alive. The, after appropriating without
acknowledgment the product of Creative Action, he proceeded to show
the remarkable instability of that product, which makes it subject
to changes under the slightest influences.

What are the nature of the changes? No one ever saw corn change
to wheat, or apples to oranges.

Sticking strictly to facts, we can accept evolution based upon
selection, adaptation, and elimination only in the sense of the
"preservation of the species." Such changes come under yearly observation. But that is the limit of evolution. These changes do not
apply to the species, but to the varieties. The appearance of new
species as transitions from other species has never been observed
anywhere.

The evidence presented here deals with the "preservation of the
species." How various species originally came into existence is a
question of Creation and not of Evolution.

But here is the loop-hole where Inductive Science, by a clever
trick, interpolates one phase to replace another, and thus deceives
him who cannot think and reason.

Having established the fact of the evolution of varieties from a
basic stock, the Evolutionist slyly applies the same evolutionary
process to the species, skilfully using the methods of analogy.

But in this particular manner, analogy is very illegitimate. And
we do not exaggerate in the least by calling it "substitution by trick,
Modern science is full of tricks. It is founded upon tricks and lives
and thrives on tricks.

The evolution of varieties is an established fact of observation. No one can deny it. But the varieties always remain within the fixed limits of the particular species, and these varieties are very instable. With the least alteration of conditions, the varieties will change after several generations, or revert to the original type.

And that is the type of instability to which Spencer referred. It is the instability of varieties and not of species.

But Spencer did not so express it. He was crafty enough to know what he was doing. He knew he was not engaged in presenting facts, but was trying to support a theory. He slyly conveyed the impression that he referred to species, not varieties. Just a trick of the prejudiced to conceal their errors.

Species is a fixed and established type; and, as stated, a change of species has never been observed and never will be. No one has ever seen corn change to wheat or monkey to man. And the so-calle missing link to fill the imaginary gap will never be found because it never existed.

Disregarding the facts of Creation, Spencer proceeded to suggest, but not to prove, that Life is the product of incidental and external forces, which by accident, perhaps is "habitually generated in all animals, save the lowest, by incident forces of every kind."

That caps the climax for stupidity and this should be remembered by the reader, when we show exactly what Nerve Force is and describe its source.

Spencer knew nothing of the nature of Nerve Force and admitted it, yet he knew where and how it originated.

If we have definite knowledge as to the origin of a force, we ipso facto have some knowledge of its nature. But up to this good day medical art knows no more about the source and nature of Nerve Force than it did two thousand years ago. Why this ignorance? It is the result of prejudice and the stubborn refusal of science to recognize the nature of the Unknowable Reality.

We are going to reveal that secret in due time, and that revelation will shock the reader. For it will present comprehensive knowledge of a great mystery. It will show the strange relationship existing between the Celestial Body and the Terrestrial body referred to in the Bible. It will explain exactly what Paul meant when he said that the first man is of the earth, earthy, but the second man is the Lord from Heaven (1 Cor. 15:40,47).

And the evidence presented will convince intelligent thinkers that the "Utterances of the Superstitious Heathens" related not to nonsense, but to a Science of Creation that has not yet been discovered by our vaunted scientists.

Life

In his process of building up his theory of Life, Spencer exhibited such doubt and hesitancy. But the point was finally reached, and the finished produce appeared in these words:

"The broadest and most complete definition of Life will be, the continuous adjustment of internal relations to external relations."

The renowned Dr. Wm. Osler came later with this statement:"Life is the expression of a series of chemical changes (in the body" (Mod. Med. 1907, p.39).

Life, as an Entity, according to these definitions, has no essential existence. Life is only a name applied to certain movements and processes of change occurring in Matter. It is just "a mode of motion." And where and what is the Power responsible for the motion? Osler held that it was chemical action. Spencer contended that the Power was a force residing in the environment.

We shall see in due time that Spencer was closer to the point. Life is a name, not an entity nor a principle. It is an effect, not a cause.

The force responsible for that "mode of motion" called Life does come from the environment. But physical science has never at any time defined and described the nature of that force. It terms the force the Unknowable Reality, then bypasses the question as unimportant.

Had the advocates of Evolution discovered the nature of that Unknowable Reality which does all and explains all, and properly traced its course of operations, their philosophy of Life and Man had been as nearly perfect as it seems possible for us to make it with our present knowledge.

Whence cometh that force which produces messages by radio and television? From the environment. Whence cometh the force which operates material bodies called animals and human beings? From the environment.

What is the nature of that force? Science calls it an Unknowable Reality and there stops.

In their failure to discover and recognize the nature of this force, and in their attempts to define and describe it, the scientists and evolutionists have committed many errors and resorted to many tricks. They realize that they are lost and try to conceal the fact by covering their course with a cloud of words.

In his First Principles, Spencer admits that "Life, as it exists in all members of such species, is an extremely complex kind of movement." He does not deny the existence of internal and intrinsical forces in Creation; but he considers that Life is unworthy of being constituted of them. He said:

"Force is the ultimate principle of existence, but Life is not such a force."

Again Spencer is right. What we do call Life is not a force but the effect of the Unknowable Reality operating within the physical organism.

Life is the term used to describe the functions of that force, which we call Vital Force, Nerve Force, Unknowable Reality. The nature and source of that force is the Universal Principle whose discovery explains everything. Emerson referred to that force in these words:

"The True Doctrine of Omnipresence is, that God reappears with all His parts in every moss and every cobweb."

Very good so far as he went, but he did not go far enough. We must define and described that God before we have the answer.

Spencer claimed that his system was Evolution. But to sustain his claim he was obliged to render his own derinition. He said:

"Evolution is an integration of Matter and concomitant dissipation of Motion, during which the Matter passes from an indefinite, incoherent homogeneity to a definite, coherent heterogeneity, and during which the retained Motion undergoes a parallel transformation."

Spencer cuts closely to the facts, but misses the Central Factors by a close shave. He also makes another miss when he holds that "the retained Motion undergoes a parallel transformation."

That explanation reveals his ignorance of the nature of the force, which he termed "the retained Motion." It does not undergo a parallel transformation. It is the most stable element in the Universe, with many phases but no changes.

The physical scientists and evolutionists regard the Universe as a product resulting from the "blind dance of atoms," which do what they do because they can do nothing else. They integrate for some unknown reason into a compound of Matter, which develops the power of movement in some mysterious way, and to this "Mode of Motion" the term Life is applied.

According to the doctrine of the physical scientists and evolutionists, there is no such entity as the Ego, the Soul, the Spirit. There is no place for these terms in their philosophy. To recognize such would require a long discussion in an attempt to show they were unworthy of consideration.

Ego is a term not found in the Bible. Paul referred to it as the Celestial Body and the Lord from Heaven. The Hindus regarded it as the Entity which inhabits the body. Paul also called it the Spirit of God. But we are still left in the dark for we are not told anything about the nature of this element, this Lord from Heaven, this Spirit of God, this Ego which inhabits the body.

Getting back to physical science, man is regarded only as a "Mode of Motion in the direction of least resistance," due to the energy inherent in food, drink, circumstances and environment. When the "motion" ceases, all is ended. That is the total extinction of Man. There is no Future Life as there is no essential present Life.

Birth begins all and Death ends all. And the peculiar concatenation of circumstances which this form of evolution produces, is the only creative power.

Spencer's arguments were so plausible that a large number of scholars, unable to swallow the supernaturalism of theology and having no other alternative, embraced his philosophy.

If every consistent philosophy must begin with the postulate of a self-existent Entity that is the source and author of all, then if congruity would be universal, every other organized system must also begin with the existence of an Entity that shall answer to all its parts.

It is what we regard as the discovery of that Cosmic Entity that has constrained us to attack the theories and doctrine of those institutions which rule our educational systems and control the Mob Mind, and to expose the errors and false conclusions of those who, by every right of position and learning, have been our teachers.

Chapter No. 5

CONFUSION

In the Bible it is written, "If a man die, shall he live again" (Job 14:14).

And in the same book it is also written: "That which thou sowest is not quickened (with new life) except it die" (1Cor. 15:36).

In these paradoxical statements both the laics and the clerics find nothing but confusion, rising from the general ignorance of physical science as to the nature of Life. How can we expect the masses of the clergy to understand when the great scientists frankly admit that they do not understand?

It appears from the biblical statements that we live to die, and we die to live. The Ancient Masters called this the Wheel of Life, and symbolized it in Card No. 10 of their Tarot.

The big question here is, What dies? What seems to die? What is Death? What does the word Death mean? What occurs when the living body sinks into a motionless state, to rise no more by its own power? What is the force which moves the body, producing that "Mode of Motion" which physical science and the evolutionists term Life? What is its nature and its source? Whence does it come? and whither does it go?

Search thru the imposing tomes of modern science for answers to these weighty questions, and none of a definite and satisfactory tone can be found. So far as science is concerned, the mystery of Life and Death is as baffling now as it was a thousand years ago. Millions of dollars and years of time are expended in research, and yet science has failed dismally to solve THE VERY FIRST PROBLEM OF HUMAN EXISTENCE.

Let the great scientists themselves speak and tell us what they know about Life. Dr. Robert A. Millikan, world renowned scientist, authority on Cosmic Rays, and late head of the California Institute wrote:

"I cannot explain why I am alive rather than dead. Physiologists can tell me much about the mechanical and chemical processes of my body, but they cannot say why I am alive" (Collier's, Oct. 24, 1925).

Dr. Alex Carrel, one of the world's greatest anthropoligists and biologist of this century, after studying Man for forty years, declared:

"Each one of us is made up of a procession of phantoms, in the midst of which (there) strides an unknowable reality. In fact, our ignorance (of the nature of Life and the constitution of Man) is profound.....

"Those (scientists)who investigate the phenomena of life are as if lost in an inextricable jungle, in the midst of a magic forest, whose countless trees unceasingly change their place and their shape..

"Cur knowledge of the human body is, in truth, most rudimentary. It is impossible, for the present, to grasp its constitution. We must, then, be content with the scientific observation of our organic and mental activities, and, without any other guide, march forward into the unknown" (Man The Unknown).

And that is the shocking state of glaring ignorance that greets us when we search thru the works of science for knowledge concerning the world's greatest mystery of what we call Life and Death. We find nothing but empty speculation and discouraging confusion.

The big publications and periodicals are filled with misleading propaganda concerning the "March of Science." But the world is not told in what direction the March is headed. The brainwashed masses are not informed that it is a blind "MARCH INTO THE UNKNOWN."

Physics and chemistry are littered with unsolved problems, and when it comes to anthropology and biology, the weakness of modern science to explain anything basic is painfully shocking.

Science possesses such a paucity of knowledge relative to these great subjects, that it was not until the recent splitting of the Atom that the mysterious nature of Creation was somewhat disclosed to the few who were competent to read the revealing signs and symbols.

And now some of the leading students of Creation have sufficient data concerning the nature of Creative Action, to enable them to understand somewhat the secret meaning of the hidden knowledge contained in the Ancient Wisdom. The Door to the Hidden Creator is beginning to open. We dimly see that the so-called foibles of antiquity are not bed-time stories for children.

We discover with astonishment that the Superstitious Heathens of the Ancient World were far ahead of our modern scientists, being inspired Seers who were truly illumined with concepts relative to the basic facts of Creation which the latest discoveries of our physical science are proving to be correct. We find now that the essence of these concepts was known ten thousand years ago, and was usually expressed in dramatical, poetical, symbolical and allegorical terms for the purpose of misleading the exoteric and confusing the profane.

Now we have the sorely needed knowledge which enables some of us to understand the great mysteries of Life and Death. Now we know what Life and Death are. Now we can identify the Unknowable Reality.

That knowledge reveals the startling secret that there is no Death in terms of extinction. There is nothing Dead. Even a stone is alive, but called Dead because its atoms vibrate below the plane where it is possible to identify animative action.

Now we know that Man actually has no body in the Death phase of Creative Action. Now we know that Death does not mean the total annihilation of Man, as stupidly taught by science and believed by its followers. Now we know what Paul meant when he said the grain which thou sowest is not quickened (with new life) except it (seems to) die.

As these startling facts regarding Life and Death dawn upon us, we are anxious to pass this knowledge on to the Man of Darkness. And we want him to remember that, while this datum is new to us, it has been the property of the Superstitious Heathens and Ignorant Pagans for thousands of years, and is really as old as the hills of time.

Life and Death

Nothing could be of more interest to Man than the subjects of Life and Death. The world's history is made up of the issues of Life and Death. All of the world's activities are shaped by the expectation of Death. Every business agreement is made under the impression that the parties thereto may not live to perform its provisions. And the gloomy uncertainty of what lies beyond this Life more or less affects the mind of every man. No individual, nor community, nor nation, escapes the shadow. It colors all acts. It enters into national policies. This certainty of Death is the "bitter drop of gall in the cup of Life." Children fear it; old age dreads it; even sickness, poverty, and crime shrink from release by Death.

The certainty of physical death conditions all life to a state of restlessness. It affects all human endeavor with a sense of impermanency. It deflects the mind from purposeful living by bringing into human thoughts the constant prospect of reaching the end. Anticipation of Death increases the apparent value of time. It creates haste and hurry. In engenders a feverish rush and struggle for early satisfaction and happiness.

It is safe to say that most men desire to live on after physical death. Most of them hope for a Future Life. Many have faith; but there are more whose hope and faith alternate with misgiving and doubt. For hope is not faith, and faith is not knowledge, yet both are inspirations to humanity. Hope is fleeting intuition, while faith is the steady expectation of the heart.

Hope for and expectation of Life beyond the grave appears to be almost inseparable from human intelligence. In this desire and expectation, the savage and the savant, the child and the adult find common ground.

Literature that has affected mankind the deepest and lasted the longest, is that which has been based upon a desire for, or an expectation or actual knowledge of, a Future Life.

The sacred scriptures of the older nations antedate secular history, and they offer hope of the Future Life. The greatest of profane writers have speculated upon the immortality of Life. The works of Plato represent a great mind inspired by a hope of Immortality, while the Psalms of the Bible represent that same hope, supported by faith. But faith is empty if not supported by fact.

It is as natural to desire Life beyond the grave, to hope for it, to seek knowledge of it, as it is to desire food and water. It is an unfortunate man who does not hope for a Future Life, and a deranged man who does not desire it. A man without hope or desire for a Future Life merely exists. He can scarcely said to be conscious of Life.

Ancient Mysteries

The universal expectation of a Future Life rises out of conditions that are definitely not physical. If the mind of man had to depend only upon physical facts and rational processes of the brain for the development of faith in a Future Life, it had never developed. For no one who has looked upon a dead body, could ever have conceived the thought of a Future Life.

It was man's desire and determination to solve the secret of Life and Death that evolved the great school of the Ancient Mysteries. That earliest effort and primal victory are prehistoric events, and yet they are scorned by science as "heathenish superstition," with no foundation in fact.

They are prehistoric events because there are no written records accessible to the general public of the work of those early schools. There are no written records in any language that can be understood. But there is a lasting record, carved on the stone temples and monuments of the ancient world, in the form of mysterious symbols and glyphs. The hidden meaning of these characters has not been understood by the modern world.

Races, nations, and continents pass into oblivion, but human effort that is worthy of retention is never wasted. Knowledge once acquired is never entirely lost. Centuries may roll into cycles and new continents may rise from the bed of the ocean, but worthy knowledge will be preserved, transmitted, and protected.

The ancient school of Metaphysical Science, while crushed by despots, has never disbanded or passed into complete oblivion. For ages its wisdom has been concealed from the eyes of the World in symbol and fable. And some advanced students, in every generation, have been competent to fathom the hidden meaning thereof. But being few in number, and their interpretation of these symbols and fables being contrary to conventional thought, their work has failed to attract much attention.

By the confinement of the Ancient Wisdom to a system of secret knowledge, guarded by the most rigid rites, could the Masters expect to preserve them from the superstitions, innovations, and corruptions of the world as it then existed.

"The distinguished few," wrote Oliver in his History of Initiation, "who retained their fidelity, uncontaminated by the contagion of evil example, would soon be able to estimate the superior benefits of an isolated institution, which afforded the advantages of a select society, and kept at an unapproachable distance the profane scoffer, whose presence might pollute their pure devotions and social converse, by contumelious language or unholy mirth."

And so, the prevention of this intrusion, and the preservation of these sublime truths, was the original object of the institution of the ceremonies of initiation, and the adoption of other means by which the initiated could be rocognized, and the uninitiated excluded.

-38-

For many years we have debated the wisdom of releasing this Ancient Wisdom to humanity in general. To accumulate the data has been our life-work. We have delved into ancient records and collected scattered and widely separated fragments of this Wisdom, gathered by researchers from the ruins of civilizations and ancient temples of the Masters,who were so far ahead of us in knowledge relating to Life and Death and the Future Life, that only a few can interpret the real meaning of the ancient symbols and allegories, and only a scattering few will accept that meaning.

The Ancient Masters understood the eternal facts that relate to Life and Death. In their symbols and allegories are hidden the references to the Universal Laws that are vaguely sensed by all men, but denied by science, missed by philosophers, scorned by doctors, and misinterpreted by theology.

Physical science augments the confusion. It enters the debate with demonstrated facts which dismay theology and disconcert metaphysics. Some of these discovered facts contradict certain theological dogmas. Physical science, therefore, declares that theology has no basis in fact. By this course it assumes that there can be no undiscovered facts which might demonstrate a Spiritual Side of Creation. Instead, physical science assumes that there are in Creation only physical facts and physical forces, and that these facts and forces are demonstrable by the methods of physical science only.

If theology really knew what it only professes to believe, very quickly would change the entire existing order of theological discourses. If physical science were able to conceive that there might be certain facts of Creation lying beyond the scope of its methods, very soon would the general scientific study and experiments include the psychic phenomena of existence. As it is, both theology and physical science agree in the conception that human intelligence cannot penetrate further into the secrets of Creation. We are going to show that this limitation is not a fact, but only a fancy and is self-imposed.

If theology could only present some logical facts to illustrate the processes of the Creative Cycle, modern thought would be transformed with new impulses and higher aspirations. If physical science could but prove its own major premise, that "all is physical matter and mechanical energy," modern theology would disintegrate within a decade.

Whereas science drives theology from one untenable position to another with its doctrine of Materialism and Evolutionism, that does not affect the basis of theology, which is faith in the accepted teachings of the law and the subconscious intuitions of humanity.

Theology woefully lacks basic knowledge of Creation and Creative Action to make a rational effort to verify its faith in a Future Life. Physical science, on the contrary, has pursued a vigorous course against what it is pleased to term the superstitions of mankind, and especially of the "ancient heathens."

It is a serious reflection upon the intelligence of modern theologians that they have failed to find the salient point of Creation which would prove the existence of the Future Life. It seems surprising that they could lack the ability to fathom the fact that since something cannot come from nothing, the Future Life could not be possible if Pre-existent life were not a positive fact.

If physical science did not stubbornly deny the importance of the Unknowable Reality, after admitting its existence, it would make a startling discovery, surpassing the discovery made relative to Matter that came with the splitting of the Atom.

The Unknowable Reality is the only Element that has absolute existence, and yet that Element is said to be Unknown and Unknowable. In that case, we, science and the world, know nothing about Absolute Existence. This means that we know nothing definite at all until we have discovered the nature of the Unknowable Reality. And if that be impossible, then man must forever live in darkness.

All questions have answers, and this question has its answer. But we cannot discover the answer to any question when we deliberately close our eyes and our mind to the facts, and stubbornly refuse to recognize the answer when it is discovered and presented to us.

Physical science has built its Edifice upon the postulate that "All is physical Matter and mechanical energy." And the scientists who live and move in that Postulate, appear to be determined not to permit anything to weaken, discredit or destroy that beloved Postulate.

To that end these scientists recklessly reject and scornfully condemn anything and everything that does not harmonize and correspond with that precious Postulate. And they quickly suppress when they show up, all facts which have an unorthodox appearance. They prefer to live and die in darkness rather than to see their shaky system of speculation disintegrate and crumble into rubble.

-40-

Herbert Spencer, one of the leading Evolutionists of the 19th century, whom we have previously noticed, said so much in his writings about the Unknowable, that one day a friend said to him, "Spencer, you know far too much about your Unknowable."

Physical science deliberately makes and claims Unknowable the one and only Universal Element that would bring the light that would banish the darkness. It takes that course because the discovery and recognition of that one and only Element would completely demolish its system of ssumption if it were permitted to become Known instead of Unknowable.

And so, physical science continues to live in the world of self-created and self-imposed darkness, while claiming that the mind of man has penetrated as far as it can go into the mystery of Creation.

Chapter No. 6

MUNDANE CREATION

It is now in order to present some real Creative Action and show what the term Creation means. The reader will observe that the facts are far different from the biblical fable regarding the creation of the world, a fable that has been accepted as factual history for sixteen hundred years by the orthodox Christians.

All bodies are created, and all created bodies have beginnings and endings. These created bodies include the earth, moon, planets, sun, stars, etc. But the Elements of which all bodies are made are uncreated and eternal. These Elements were postulated by the Ancient Masters for the purpose of convenience, as Fire, Air, Water, and Earth, the Sacred Four, represented in the Ancient Scriptures by the letters J H V H, a preposition so important that to it a later chapter will be devoted.

We refer to the Bible for the first hint of Mundane Creation, as Laplace (1748-1827) no doubt did, when he formulated his Nebular Cosmogony Hypothesis.

It would seriously detract from the power of scientific prestige for a scientist to admit the discovery of any valuable data in the Scriptures of the Superstitious Heathens. And so, the scientists very discretly keep such things hidden, and especially those scientists who scorn the suggestion of a Creative Power.

In symbol and fable definite reference to Nebular Cosmogony appears in the Bible, which describes in the book of Ezekiel (1) the Nebula, (2) the Four Elements, (3) and the Earth.

The Nebula is said to be a Cloud of Fire, the Prima Materia of the Universe. The Four Elements are symbolized as Four Beasts; and the Earth is referred to as Wheels.

In the Bible it is said that Ezekiel the priest, the son of Buzi, in the land of the Chaldeans by the river Cheoar, "looked, and behold, a whirlwind came out of the north, a great cloud, and a fire infolding itself, and a brightness was about it, and out of the midst thereof as the color of amber, out of the midst of the fire"(Ezek. 1:4).

This Ezekiel states that he was in Chaldea. That was the land of the great astronomers of the world at that time. What he saw in his vision and described in his writings was a recital of what he discovered in the Chaldean scrolls that dealt with Mundane Creation. Just another one of those clever tricks with which the history of the world is filled, and most especially the Bible.

The author of the last book of the Bible had a vision too, "and heard behind me a great voice, as of a trumpet, saying, I am Alpha and Omega, the first and the last; and what thou seest, write in a book, and sent it unto the seven churches (synagogues) which are in Asia" (Minor).

The author then proceeds to prepare one of the most stupendous allegories ever penned by the hand of man, so profound in context that it has puzzled the best brains of the Christian World for sixteen hundred years, and still remains an unsolved enigma.

Some day the orthodox Christians may know something about the essence of their Bible. Then they will know who wrote Revelation, and where that ancient scroll originated. It came from India, and it was originally written several thousand years before the world ever heard of the gospel Jesus. The version in the Bible was edited to make it harmonize with the conditions of the Jews in Palestine.

In the Chaldean scroll Ezekiel perused the account of the whirling nebular of Incandescent Gas out of which Laplace formed the Universe.

Ezekiel mentioned the Four Elements as Four Beasts, which are used all thru the Bible to Symbolize the Four Elements of which all Creation is constituted, according to the Ancient Masters.

These Four Beasts also represent the four fixed signs of the Zodiakos, the Lion (Fire), the Eagle (Air), the Angel (Water), and the Bull (Earth).

The Wheels described by Ezekiel (1:5) refer to the Zodiakos, which was designed by the Ancient Masters to represent the World (Earth). The World is also the subject of Tarot Card No. 21, the symbolism of which we have interpreted and discussed in another work titled "The Land Of Light."

The Sphinx is constituted of the Four Beasts mentioned in the Bible, and this image is so old that it is found in all the ancient nations on Earth. It is the Great Symbol of the Four Elements, and

this symbolism applies to every kind of cosmic force, substance and
element of the Universe, from the primordial element of Fire to the
Supreme Intelligence of the Creator, as we have shown in another
work titled "The Mysterious Sphinx."

As stated, the Wheels refer to the Zodiakos, the little one and
the large one, the smaller one representing the annual cycle of the
Sun thru its twelve signs, whereas the larger represents the whole
solar system which passes thru the Twelve Constellations once every
25,868 years, according to data built in to the Great Pyramid of
Gizeh.

Presession of the Equinoxes

The exceedingly ancient knowledge of the Precession of the
Equinoxes was lost for ages, due to the work of ancient despots in
the destruction of knowledge. It was partially recovered in 125 B.
C. by the Greek Astronomer Hipparchus. But he was not able to explain the purpose of the larger cycle. And the modern world has
been so ignorant of Cosmic Science, that it had to wait eighteen
hundred years for the great mind of Sir Isaac Newton to fathom the
mystery and determine the cause of this cosmic action, which knowledge the Superstitious Heathens possessed ten thousand years ago.

The time required for the earth to make a complete revolution
in its orbit around the Sun is roughly 365.25 days. In determining
the length of the year, we disregard the odd quarter day, and give
the year the round number of 365 days for three successive years,
and every fourth year 366 days. and this is called "leap year."

When a peg top spins, it wobbles on its axis. So does the earth.
This wobble results in the North Pole rotating in a small circle, so
that it points to a new part of the sky as time passes. This movement, called Precession, is not great enough for us to detect casual-
ly, for a single rotation requires 25,868 years, as stated. As a
consequence of Precession, the position of the Arctic and Antarctic
Circles are gradually changing.

The Precession of the Equinoxes is a retrograde motion in the
passage of the Sun as it annually crosses the ecliptic. The Equinox
was calculated by the Ancient Astrologers to move at the rate of 1
degree in 72 years.

This movement makes the place of the Sun, at the beginning of
the astronomical year, appear to retrograde thru the Zodiakos 1 degree
in 72 years, completeing the circle about 72 x 360 degrees, equal
25,920 years, or 25,868 to be exact.

-44-

This cycle of 360 degrees is divided by 12 into sections corresponding to the Zodiakal Signs, each section containing 30 degrees. When we divide 25,868 by 12 the result is approximately 2,155 years as the duration of one subcycle, or an Age as it is called, the Piscean Age, the Aquarian Age, etc.

Thus will it be observed that it required a vast period of time for the Ancient Astrologers to check and recheck this data thru the ages, compare it and formulate their chart and prepare their record, describing not .only these mysteries of Creative Action, but also the condition of the Earth and its inhabitants, as affected by the vibrations of the various Celestial Bodies symbolized in the Zodiakos. And this marvelous data the dictionaries, histories and encyclopedias, prepared under the censorship of prejudiced men who hate the Ancient Heathens, declare are false, counterfeit and spurious, being nothing more than the twaddle of Superstitious Heathens.

There is one hidden reason for this prejudice, and here we are going to reveal it: The scribe of the John gospel made his Jesus say, "In my Father's house are many mansions.....I go to prepare a place for you. And if I go and prepare a place for you, I will come again" (John 14:2,3).

These many mansions in my Father's house are the celestial houses of the Zodiakos, and this Jesus at this time and point symbolized the head-sign of the Zodiakos, and as such, he would "come again" in 25,868 years, and then would reign 2,155 years.

The mystery passages in the Bible have a distinct meaning, and the answers to them were known to the Ancient Astrologers and to the men who compiled the Bible from the Scrolls of these Astrologers.

According to modern science, the Earth was born of and in a huge cloud of incandescent gas, glowing with intense heat--that Cloud of Fire mentioned in the Bible and the data scooped from the scrolls of the ancient Chaldeans.

Science says that our entire solar system evolved from that gigantic cloud of incandescent, electrified gas, of enormous proportions, such as the giant telescopes show are scattered by the thousands throughout the great reaches of space.

Our Sun, a star, is one of the thousands of millions of stars that constitute the Milky Way, so-called because the millions of stars make it so brilliant, and which is so large that it staggers the imagination. It is constituted of about fifty million times the number of stars that we can see on the darkest of nights.

This mighty mass of suns of the Milky Way and our own galaxy, are just part of the visible Universe. It is part of a local group that includes some sixteen or more star systems. And yet this local group extends over an area so vast, that it takes two million years for light to cross it at a speed of more than 186,000 miles a second.

This local group is but a dwarf cluster. In the vast reaches of endless space there are gigantic clusters of galaxies, composed not of a few members as our own is, but sometime five hundred of them----whole galaxies of galaxies, which make our own local group seem insignificant.

The particular Nebula that gave birth to our own little solar system, contracted and condensed, as it whirled at great speed thru space, and, in so doing, wobbled as it went, leaving behind at irregular intervals huge masses of congealing gas that subsequently formed the planets of our solar system, according to science, of which the earth is one. But this is an assumption which is said to be open to question.

Our local sun is a tremendous body of glowing hot substance, in size some 700 times more massive than the combined mass of the planets of our solar system, but very small when compared to the great red giant Antares, which has 400 times the candlepower of our sun, and is over 450 times its diameter, its mass being some hundreds of thousands of that of our sun.

So hot is the sun's atmosphere, that stone, steel, and all the various metalic substances are present in it in a state of glowing hot gas. These substances are the same as those which constitute the earth and everything on it, including the mineral, vegetal, animal and humanal kingdoms.

Here is a big point to remember. For the time comes when the earth is formed and covered with everything known, and mystery rises as to their nature, origin and constitution. Here in the glowing hot gases of the Universe are the nature, origin and constitution of everything known, including Man. Out of the fiery gases he came and to them he returns. From Fire to Fire is the law. Follow us and learn in due time the strange facts of the mysterious Fiery Man.

It is the triumph of the spectroscope, in the light of scientific knowledge, to have demonstrated that at this time there are in existence other giant masses of gaseous substance, from which other planets, suns and stars are constantly being evolved. When their surfaces shall have cooled sufficiently, they will become the home of living things just as our earth has.

The Igneous Age

In the initial state of the Earth, it was for millions of years
a ball of white-hot substance. That was the Igneous or Sun Age of
the Earth.

Every newly created celestial body is first a ball of glowing
hot substance, and begins to cool as it condenses. This means that
every celestial body is at first a Sun, and becomes a planet millions
of years later when it has had time to cool.

According to science, the course is from incandescent gas, to
sun, planet, moon, comet, asteriod, dust, and incandescent gas
again. That is another phase of the Creative Cycle which affects
everything.

Science says this is the life-history of a cosmic body, a matter
of three or four billion years, we are told. Compared to theology,
that is bold and daring, but compared to factology, it is as mild as
theology and just as timid. For this earth, as an entity, is old
beyond our wildest dreams---a matter of trillions of years.

The ancient Hindus were aware of this fact, and asserted that
from chaos back to chaos is a matter of some 311,000,000,000,000 years.
That's more like it.

How long did it take for the earth to cool and become a home for
living things? In 1862 Lord Kelvin computed the time required for
the earth to cool from a temperature of 3000 degrees C. to its present temperature, assuming the recognized law of heat radiation to
have prevailed unchanged in principle during that time. The answer
came out as 30,000 years.

It was later determined that Kelvin began with too cool a temperature. It should have been 5000 degrees C. This would make a corresponding increase in the length of time required for the earth to cool
to its present temperature, or approximately 52,5000,000 years.

This means that it was more than fifty million years after the
earth was born, before its surface was cool enough to become a home
for living things. During most of that time the earth was a blazing
sun, far larger than it is now. For as it cooled in temperature it
shrank in size, and grew more dense. A ball of cotton a yard in
diameter may be only an inch in diameter when compressed to the den-
sity of steel.

The earth's center is still a mass of glowing-hot substance. As
it cools it shrinks, and the gases generated by the internal heat
escape thru volcanic pores in the surface or crust. As the earth

cools more and shrinks more and the outer crust thickens more, it will grow more difficult for the internal gases to escape. And the time will come, says science, in some billions of years hence, when these accumulated and confined gases will cause the earth to explode like a gigantic bomb. As the fragments of the exploded globe then fly thru space at terrific speed, the intense friction resulting will reduce the fragments to dust, and the substance of which the earth was composed, will return again to the cosmic reservoir as incandescent gas.

The press of August 22, 1961, announced that a giant star exploded in space about 300 million years ago, and the light of that explosion, some 100 to 1000 million times brighter than our sun, has just reached our earth, traveling at a speed of 136,000 miles a second.

This report came from Dr. Fritz Zwicky of Mt. Palomar Observatory in California. He sighted the brilliant light two months ago, within a few days after the flash arrived.

And thus do all created bodies have their origins and terminations, regardless of whether they are stars, suns, planets, trees, or animals, the only difference being the length of time they last.

The Boiling Sea

As the ages passed, the surface of the young sun cooled, and the surrounding incandescent gases condensed, forming a huge mass of dark clouds, incessantly pierced by shafts of lighning, accompanied by crashing peals of thunder.

Rain fell from the clouds, but before it could reach the hot sun, the drops were vaporized by the heat, and the vapor rose high as clouds, to condense and fall again as rain when the cooling air miles above made the clouds too heavy to float.

This creative action continued for millions of years before the sun cooled down enough to receive the rain. As the rain at last reached the surface of the sun, that was cooling down to become a planet, the water formed into pools which filled the fissures in the hardened lava. The water was boiling hot and from its surface huge clouds of vapor rose like steam from a gigantic caldron.

This creative action continued for millions of years before the sun cooled sufficiently to stop heating to the boiling point the water that rippled over its laval surface.

-48-

As the newly created sun continued to cool to take its place
as a planet, the rain continued to fall, and the pools grew larger,
until the whole surface of the newly created planet was covered by
a shallow sea of scalling water. The water of this primitive ocean
gradually cooled until living things could endure the heat--and at
last the new-born planet that began as a sun, became the home of
living things.

Chapter No. 7

CREATIVE ACTION

As we Hunt for the Hidden Creator we search for our goal in the
mystery of Creation, the term defined by the dictionary as "The act
of creating (something) from nothing."

In referring to Creation, a noted author said, "It is a process
by the means of which Substance is transformed in such manner as to
be caused to conform to the specifications of a definite plan.
Reasoning from this definition, it becomes obvious that every creative
act involves two indispensable factors, viz;, a Creator and a Substance."

He continued: "The absence of either of these factors automatically renders Creation impossible. In the absence of a Creator,
Substance must remain an inert mass; and in the absence of Substance,
the Creator must remain sterile, because He has nothing with which
to exercise His Creative Powers. In other words, something is never
created from nothing; and no Creation of any kind is possible without a Creator to do the creating.

Then he made this shrewd observation: "There are two popular
fallacies of Creation which serve as stumbling-blocks to most sincere
persons who attempt to gain and apply an understanding of Creative
Action. One is the theory that Creation is the mystic art of making
something out of nothing. The other is the materialistic concept
that Creation is a haphazard and spontaneous process which operates
without a motivating power to do the work, and without a guiding intelligence to direct the process. Both of these presumptions are
logically indefensible myths. They have no basis in fact, and serve
only to increase the confusion of the unwary."

The foolishness and worthlessness of these two fallacies, taught
in our schools and colleges, are the reasons why college graduates
in the Christian World are incompetent to analyze intelligently the
basic principles of Creative Action.

One of these fallacies is taught by theology, which adheres
strictly to the literal statements of the Bible, and teaches children
as positively true the process of Creation set forth in the first
chapter of Genesis, and they grow up steeped in that fallacy.

Then comes the fallacy of science, opposed to this one and taught the children in the schools, to the effect that the world is composed of blind and unknown forces; that we are nothing but infinitely small particles on the surface of a grain of dust in the immensity of the cosmos; that this cosmos is totally deprived of Life and Consciousness, and that our Universe is exclusively chemical and mechanical, since it has been created from an unknown substratum by the techniques of physics and mechanics.

Between these two popular fallacies, one based on an ancient fable that appears in the Bible, and the other based on the wild speculations of science, the actual facts of Creation run a terrible gauntlet in this bewildered world of mental darkness.

The historical researches of Copernicus, Kepler and Newton were inspired by a deep desire to solve the mystery of Creation. They opinionated that they could discover something definite concerning the Creator by learning more about the Universe which he had made according to the account of Creation contained in the Bible.

The net result of this research was very disappointing, and is related by Dr. Andrew D. White in these words:

"There came, one after the other, five of the greatest men of modern times--Copernicus, Kepler, Descartes, Newton and Laplace--and when their work was done, the biblical concept of the Creation of the Universe (by the fiat of a Creator as stated in the Bible) was exploded and gone."

Dr. White was careful not to include in this "explosion" the fallacy of the scientific concept of Creation. His shots were aimed exclusively at the theological fallacy of Creation presented in the Bible; and he may have believed himself in the fallacy of the scientific postulate of Creation. For unto this day that fallacy is taught as a solid fact in the schools and colleges.

One of the reasons for the lack at the present time of basic data relative to Anthropology, Biology, Psychology, Physiology and Pathology, rises from the fact that for at least a century a materialistic science, which stubbornly denies the existence of a Spiritual World and just as stubbornly contends that "all is physical matter and mechanical energy," has been elevated to the status of a religion.

"Genesis is not in it with a school text-book on chemistry," said Prof. J.H. Woodger. This scientific dogmatism dates from the days of our grandfathers who believed the Universe is a gigantic machine made of hard, solid, invisible atoms.

Then something most startling happened--the splitting of that hard, solid, invisible atom. Concerning this remarkable event one author observes:

"The splitting of the Atom was the great achievement of this age, supplying the sort of below the surface knowledge we needed in all things. Until we apply that knowledge to all things, including religion, we are but superficialists groping about in worlds not realized. Knowledge of matter's real nature is something that Nature has waited, perhaps eons, for man to achieve. For it marks the turning point in the long, descending process of the Planetary Night, the process from here on being upward."

According to Prof. Eddington, the result of this achievement transformed "the eternal world of physics into a world of shadows, and left science dangling from a limb."

Prof. J. S. Haldane, the great astronomer. said: "Materialism, once a plausible theory (of science) is now the fatalistic creed of thousands (of scientists), but materialism is nothing better than a superstition, on the same level as a belief in witches and devils. The materialist theory is backrupt."

Prof. A.N. Whitehead made this shrewd observation: "The progress of Science has now reached a turning point. The stable foundations of Physics have been exploded....The old foundations of scientific thought are becoming unintelligible (and they are still taught in the schools). Time, space, matter, material, ether, electricity, mechanism, organism, configuration, structure, pattern, function,--all these require reinterpretation. What's the sense of talking about a mechanical explanation (of the Universe when you don't know what you mean by mechanics" (Science and the Modern World).

And thus goes science out the window, along with its baseless assumptions and wild speculations concerning the world (that) is composed of blind and unknown forces, and a Universe that "is exclusively mechanical."

The amazing feature which was discovered by the five great men mentioned by Dr. White, was the surprising fact that the Universe is a self-creating, self-generating Unit, working constantly and automatically in an intelligent manner, possessing both the Power and the Substance to do all that it needs to do, with no cause for any additional assistance from any source, not even from science or theology.

For the benefit of both the laics and the clerics, we shall analyze some phases of the Creative Processes discovered by the five great men referred to by Dr. White:--

1. A decrease in temperature automatically changes invisible vapor to water which falls as rain, creating lakes and streams. A further fall in temperature changes water to ice of such strength, that it will sustain the weight of elephants, thus presenting to the mind a picture of giant animals standing on invisible vapor. That is Creation in action.

2. We plant a little lifeless-looking seed of an apple in the ground, where it is moistened by the rain and warmed by the sun, and it produces a tree that bears apples, under the law of sameness that like begets like. The required intelligence to observe the law is inherent in the seed. That is Creation in action.

3. Nothing appears more lifeless than a hen's egg, as previously mentioned in Chapter 1. After a few weeks of brooding, the apparently lifeless substance of the egg changes into a living chick that steps forth into the world, endowed with sufficient strength and intelligence to take care of its needs, and to supply itself with everything required to sustain it in accordance with the law of its being. That is Creation in action.

4. Creation's greatest work is the making of Man. It uses the body of the human mother as its workshop, and builds the body of man by the materialization of radiant elements. In due time that new body is ready to emerge from the mother's body, and be born into the world, a living being. That is Creation in action.

Gestation is the process of Creation that occurs in the mother's womb, and this process is the work of Creative Action and not of the mother. Nor does the substance which builds the body come from the mother; for Creation does not build New Bodies of used, second-hand material. That building element, as stated above, is condensed cosmic radiation, the same as that of which all objects are created.

In all of the four cases of Creative Action mentioned above, we witness a regular, intelligent order of work, appearing as an automatic process that is activated by the Condition of the environment.

Colonel James Churchward observed these facts, and wrote: "Under the great law of Creation, there must first come a Condition (of the environment), and with it (there comes) a suitable life (organism) to live in it." Then he added:

"Throughout the entire history of the earth, this has been so; and at no time do we find a new Creation behind the Condition, because the Condition is the Parent of the Creation" (Lost Continent of Mu, p. 328).

The Condition, while being absolutely essential, is not actually the Parent of The Creation. The Condition is the requirement that sets in motion the automatic process of Creative Action.

And where is the Creator while all this Creative Action is occurring ? Is He sitting on a golden throne in space, producing the product by word of mouth and wave of hand as stated in the biblical fable?

He is not. On the contrary, the Creator is the Universal Power that does the work, and the Bible says that in this Power we live, and move, and have our being (Acts 17:28).

When the compilers of the Bible permitted that vital data to slip by them and get into their book, along with some other telling statements which we shall select from the Bible and present in due time, they unwittingly preserved for us from the valuable scrolls that were burnt, some of the most important and precious scraps of the Ancient Wisdom.

What is that Universal Power? What is its nature and its source? Who has defined it and informed us? Here is the great mystery. The Ancient Masters described it, and that data appears in the Bible. Who is competent to pick it out? We are at the Door To The Hidden. The prospects appear promising. We've found the hay-stack. Now all we have to do is to find the proverbial needle. Can we do it? Can it be done?

All of the five great men whose remarkable researches exploded the biblical concept of the Creation of the Universe, failed to find it. And when it eluded them so completely, they concluded that it did not exist.

Then science steps in and attempts to fill the gap by claiming that it is nothing more than blind,mechanical energy. That dogma rules our schools, and also the medic who administers poison to a sick man in an attempt to change the function of his body. If he dies, the disease killed him; if he lives, the poison saved him.

The mystery of Creation was not solved by the great men whose findings exploded the biblical concept of Creation. That mystery will not be solved until there has been discovered and presented some-

-54-

understandable knowledge of every element involved in Creative Action. And of all the various elements engaged in the process, there is none so vital and important as the Power that does the actual work.

The Universal Power that performs all Creative Action is the basic proposition that remains unsolved. Theology calls it God,which simply pushes the mystery back another notch without explaining anything. And science calls it blind, mechanical energy and regards that as final.

Dr. Alexis Carrel, one of the great scientists of this century, said:

"Man is made up of a procession of phantoms, in the midst of which there strides an Unknowable Reality" (Man The Unknown).

The same philosophy applies without exception to every living creature, to every tree and every plant. It is the mystery of that Unknowable Reality which scientists rapidly bypass in their imposing discussions; and not even the great Carrel dared to pause at that point and make a definite attempt to analyze that mysterious quality. But he did include this frank and edifying admission:

"Our knowledge of the human body is, in truth, most rudimentary. In fact, our ignorance is profound. Most of the questions put to themselves by those (scientists) who study human beings remain without answer. Immense regions of man's inner world are still unknown. It is impossible, for the present, to grasp its constitution. We must, then, be content with the scientific observation of our organic and mental activities, and, without any other guide, march forward into the unknown" (Man The Unknown).

This is the admitted state of ignorance that prevails in the realm of pathology, yet we are blandly assured by those engaged in the work that within a comparatively short time "disease" will be completely eradicated, provided, however, that the money for the research work required will continue to pour into the medical coffers.

And this admitted state of ignorance, concerning the most vital element in all Creation, is heralded in big publications and periodicals as "The March of Science." Now we know the direction of that proud "march." Carrel told us in the above remarks, and he goes further in these words:

"Those (scientists) who investigate the phenomena of Life, are as if lost in an inextricable jungle, in the midst of a magic forest, whose countless trees unceasingly change their place and their shape" (Man The Unknown).

Dr. White was justified in his statement that the biblical concept of the Creation of the Universe by the fiat of God was exploded and gone.

But we must not forget the fact that the work of Dr. White's great men did not disclose the deep secret of Creation. Their findings exploded the biblical concept without replacing it with anything definite on that point. And so, we are very little better off now than we were before those great men "took their turn at bat."

Pursing the trail of physical science in all things, we are constantly brought to a line which, we are assured, cannot be passed --"the-ring-pass-not." Beyond that limit lies the great Unknown, and further advance in that dark realm is impossible--for science says so.

We accept this data as evidence not of the inability of man to advance to a knowledge of higher causes, but of the inadequacy of the method of research that has been followed and conducted by science All questions have answers, and with an adequate system of scientific research, it is possible to ascend to higher levels where these answers lie hidden, and to progress laterally without any limit.

The further we follow a false philosophy, the denser grows the nature of the unknown, and the more uncertain we become at each step. But the dogma of the Creation by the fiat of God has failed to satisfy active minds of deeper discernment.

Law, order, system and development are so intimately related and conjoined, that the thinking mind will not bring its searchings to an end, and rest its reasonings upon the belief, that God, without the observance of law and order as revealed by all Created Phenomena, by word of mouth and wave of hand, commanded into existence out of nothing, the countless formations of the majestic Universe.

Chapter No. 8

TETRAGRAMMATON

The Tetragrammaton and the Sphinx form a pair of the best symbols in all ancient literature as examples which reveal the clever methods used by the learned Masters to confound the exoteric and instruct the esoteric.

In the entire Bible there is nothing more clever, and yet nothing more confusing, than the introductory passage in the John Gospel, to the effect that,--

"In the beginning (of what?) was the Word (meaning what?), and the Word was (not only) with God, but (more startling) the Word was God."

This definitely states that God is a Word. That appears to contradict all previous biblical statements relative to God's nature. No one is able to make sense out of that statement without a clear understanding of the nature and the meaning of this mysterious WORD that is God. And to him who knows the hidden meaning of the WORD, every word in the above passage is absolutely a factuality, as we shall show in this discussion.

When the secret meaning of this WORD was lost, it is amazing to observe how it flourished and grew into the mysterious Logos of the theologians, who were utterly ignorant of its basic meaning. And many are the imposing, ill-informed authors who have written books to expose their ignorance of the nature of the WORD, in their attempts to explain its meaning. And that basic meaning, when known, can be presented in one short sentence.

This same general rule runs regularly and constantly thru all ancient scriptures, such as the Talmud and the Kabala,--the Practical Kabala, the Literal Kabala, and the Dogmatic Kabala.

This Kabalistic Confusion, as it should be called, was the building of a mountain out of a mole-hill, and employed by the Masters in the edification of the Neophyte in the mysteries of Creation, of the Universe, of Man, his nature, and his relation-ship to the Creator, explaining why Man passed from spiritual to material conditions, and how he may, by partaking of the Tree of Good and Evil, ultimately regain his spiritual estate, and also partake of the Tree of Life, and so attain Self-Conscious Immor-tality,-- just as if these cosmic conditions were not automatic and had to be acquired by secret processes taught by the scheming priest-hood.

As it required much time and toil to produce that darkness, so it will require much time and toil to dissipate that darkness. But it is more difficult to lead Man to the Light than to let him sink into darkness. For the sinking is much easier. It requires no ef-fort. We just float with the current and down we go.

Tetragrammaton is a Greek compound, found in Philo and Josephus, and means The Word Of Four Letters. The letters appear as J H V H. The biblical compilers, who knew the real meaning of that WORD, wove these letters into the narrative covering the interview between the Biblical God and the Biblical Moses, relative to the Children of Israel, a mythical tribe unknown beyond the Bible.

"And the Lord spake unto Moses face to face, as a man speaketh unto his friend, ...and said unto him, I am the Lord: and I appeared unto Abraham, and unto Isaac, and unto Jacob, by the name of God the Almighty (El Shaddai), but by the name of JeHoVaH was I not known to them" (Ex. 6:2,3; 33:11).

Now listen to what the Encyclopedia Britannica (13th ed.) says: "The derivation and pronunciation of the Tetragrammaton is still doubtful. The form 'JeHoVaH' used in the English Versions is an error that arose in the 16th century....The Jews called the Tetragram-maton by a Hebraic denomination, Shem Rammophorash, i.e., the distinc-tive excellent name. It was considered an act of blasphemy for a

layman to pronounce the Tetragrammaton. This avoidance of the
original name was due on the one hand to reverence and on the other
to fear lest the name be desecrated by heathens. Partly in consequence of this mystery and partly in accord with the prevalent
superstition, the Tetragrammaton figures in magical formulae from
the time of the Gnostics, on amulets. Many a medieval miracle-
worker was supposed to derive his competence from this knowledge
of the secret Name."

Coulson Turnbull tried to define the WORD in his Solar Logos.
He said:

"The Logos is and interprets cosmic force; it is life, sensation; it is man's reason; it is his prescience, intuition and inspira-
tion" (p.7).

The Sacred WORD, the Logos, is all that and more; but the basic
meaning, the essence, of the Logos was unknown to these authors. That
is the case with those who, since the days of Plato and Philo, have
written volumes on the Logos. Some may have known the secret, but
did not dare reveal it.

The Masons have their mysterious WORD. The mythical history of
Free-masonry states that there once existed a WORD of surpassing
value, and claiming a profound veneration; that this WCRD was known
to but few; that it was at length lost; and that a temporary substitution for it was adopted.

The Encyclopedia of Freemasonry says:"As the very philosophy
of Masonry teaches us that there can be no death without a resurrec-
tion--no decay without a restoration--on the same principle it follows
that the loss of the WORD must suppose its eventual recovery" (Vol. 1,
p. 453).

And to this day the Masons are still searching for the Lost
WORD.

The Sacred Four

In his book titled The Sacred Symbols of Mu (Lemuria), Col.
James Churchward wrote: "The Sacred Four is among the oldest relig-
ious conceptions. I found it in the Sacred Inspired Writings of
Mu" (Lemuria).

According to tradition, Mu (Lemuria) was a land that sank in
the sea thousands of years ago, and that from it there spread to various regions of the earth the knowledge of Creation that the Lemurian

Masters had discovered after ages of study and observation.

A great mystery appears to surround The Sacred Four, and Four is often mentioned in many ways in the Bible.

The Holy City is laid Four Square; the mystical White Stone (Cube of Space) is square; there are Four Cardinal Points, North, South, East and West, presided over by Four Great Angels, Michael, Raphael, Gabriel, and Phannel; there are Four Gospels in the New Testament; there are the Four Sacred Beasts of Ezekiel, Daniel and Revelation.

The Pythagoreans called Four "the great miracle; a God after another manner, a manifold; the foundation of Nature; the Key-Bearer of Nature," etc. In Genesis there are Four Mystical Rivers represented as watering the Garden of Eden.

In his collection of ancient tablets, over 12,000 years old, discovered by Niven in Mexico, he found written on some, "The Sacred Four," the "Four Great Pillars," the "Four Great Architects," the "Four Great Builders," and the "Four Powerful Ones" (Symbols of Mu, p. 74).

The Sphinx

One of the most peculiar symbols, found in all countries of the ancient world, is the Sphinx. For data on this symbol we consulted both the Britannica and Americana Encyclopedias, and find that those who wrote in them about the Sphinx, knew no more about the true meaning of its symbolism than the man in the moon. They said:

"A mythological monster variously described....The Sphinx, in the mythology of ancient Egypt, represented the Solar Deity, Ra... All nations of antiquity seem to have held these monstrous beings of various shapes and forms as objects of awe, compelling adoration and worship."

The Arabian Traveller and Historian, Abdullatif (1162-1231 A.D.), in referring to the Sphinx of Gizeh, wrote:

"At a little more than an arrow's flight from the pyramids is a colossal figure of a head and neck projecting from the sand; the name of the figure is 'Father of Terrors.'

"In spite of its enormous size, everything was in proportion to nature....In a face of such colossal size, how the sculptor could have been able to preserve the exact proportions of every part, seeing that nature presented him with no model of a similar colossus, or anything at all comparable."

We thus learn that as late as the 13th century A.D., the Sphinx at Gizeh, regarded as the Father of Terrors, was still buried up to its neck in the wind-blown sand of the desert, just as it was when first found by the Egyptians. They were at a loss to know what it was or what it represented.

It seems strange that no definite data of the Sphinx appears in the Bible, for the image was hoary with age before the first scrolls of the Bible were written. The Bible often mentions Four Beasts, but the exoteric never suspect they are the four aspects of the Sphinx.

Ezekiel saw a whirlwind come out of the north, a great cloud of fire infolding itself....and out of the midst thereof came the likeness of four living creatures. Then follows a sensational description of the Sphinx, mixed up then with the Zodiakos, the description of which is just as sensational (Chap. 1: 4,5,15-21 Ezekiel).

Daniel saw strange things in a vision. The four winds of heaven strove upon the great sea (Mediterranean), and four great beasts came up from the sea. Then he recites a sensational description of the Sphinx.

In Revelation mention is made of four beasts round about the throne, and then follows a description of the Sphinx.

We are going to learn as we proceed why the Sphinx plays such a leading role in the Ancient Scriptures.

Thousands of years ago the Lemurians invented symbols to conceal their discoveries of the mysteries of Creation, using them as charts in the work of teaching their disciples. Only within recent times have advanced students of occultism and Creation been competent to interpret the true meaning of some of these ancient symbols.

The land now called Egypt had been visited by certain Masters from Lemuria, and there they built the Great Pyramid of Gizeh and constructed the Sphinx.

An inscription of the 4th dynasty, extending back 4000 years before the dawn of Christianity, mentions the Sphinx then as being a monument so ancient, that its origin and meaning were lost in the night of time, and that it had been discovered by accident, buried in the sand, beneath which it has stood forgotten for ages unknown.

The Great Pyramid and the Sphinx are so old, that when the people known in history as the ancient Egyptians, settled in the valley of the Nile, they found these structures almost buried in the desert sand. It took years of labor to dig the sand away from them, and when the work was finished, the Sphinx was found to be 189 feet long, and carved from solid stone. The face of the Sphinx looks to the East, and it was called the Image of Harmakuti, or the Sun of the Horizon.

There is a tradition to the effect that the Sphinx is a complex hieroglyph, or Book in Stone, to contain the essence of the Ancient Wisdom, and reveals its message to him who can interpret this strange cipher which is embodied in the forms, correlations and measurements of the various parts of the image. That is the famous riddle of the Sphinx which, from the most ancient times, many wise men have attempted to solve.

The Light of the Great Facts of Creation is too bright for the eyes of him who has not been prepared for them, and especially when he sees them for the first time. There is danger in new discoveries which suddenly appear unexpectedly. Many are they who will read these pages and reject the knowledge they contain, because of its sudden appearance and great simplicity.

The Sphinx, with its riddle, expressed the same thought. Legend said that it devoured those who approached it and could not solve its message.

In other words, those who discovered in the symbolism of the Sphinx the mystery of God and Creation, could never again live as they had before.

The mystery surrounding the Sacred WORD and the Sphinx was unfolded by a man who has been called the Last of the Great Magicians. He was a gifted personage who lived in Paris in the last century and wrote under the pseudonym of Eliphas Levi. This remarkable man was Alphonse Louis Constant, a French Priest who was always on the edge of the excommunication and even worse because of his flaunting of papal authority. In his History of Magic (1853) he revealed the essence of the Sacred WORD, showing that it was embodied in the symbolism of the Sphinx. He wrote:

"The universal Key of magical works is that of all ancient religious dogmas--the Key of the Kabala and the Bible, the Little Key of Solomon.

"This Clavicle, regard for centuries as lost, has been recovered by us, and with it we have been able to open the sepulchres of antiquity, to make the dead speak, to behold the monuments of the past in all their glory, to understand the enigmas of the Sphinx, and to penetrate all sanctuaries (of the ancient world).

"Among the ancients, the use of the Key was permitted to none but the high priest, and even so, its secret was confined only to the flower of the Initiates....This was the Key in question: A hieroglyphic and numeral alphabet, expressing by symbols and numbers a series of universal and absolute ideas (concerning Creation)....

"The symbolical tetrad, represented in the (Egyptian) Mysteries of Memphis and Thebes by the four forms of the Sphinx,--man, eagle, lion and bull--corresponded with the Four Elements of antiquity (Fire, Air, Water and Earth).

"These four (astrological) signs, with all their analogies, explain the one (Sacred) WORD hidden in all (ancient)Sanctuaries.... Moreover, the Sacred WORD was never pronounced; it was always spelt, and expressed in four words, which are the Four Sacred Words Yod-He-Vau-He" (usually written J H V H)--Transcendental Magic.

The vowelization in the Bible of the initial letters J H V H was another clever disguise adopted to conceal from the profane and exoteric the secret of the Sacred Four. It is just one of many such instances in the Bible which we could indicate.

In the primary stage the Sacred Four related to the Four Elements of the Macrocosm that constitute all created bodies. In their secondary stage they related to the Four Principal Glands of the Microcosm involved in creative processes, as follows:

1. Pineal, Fire (Animative), top center of brain
2. Pituitary, Air (Intelligence), lower center of brain
3. Prostate, Water (Creative Fluid), base of solar plexus
4. Gonads, Earth (Procreative), base of spine.

These correspond with the Four Fixed Signs of the Zodiakos, Leo, Scorpio, Aquarius, and Taurus. These Four each take three signs or Gates, namely, a positive, a negative, and a balance sign in the center, which can be tabulated as follows:

Fire	Water	Air	Earth
Aries	Cancer	Libra	Capricorn
Leo	Scorpio	Aquarius	Taurus
Sagittarius	Pisces	Gemini	Virgo

In the Bible these are mentioned as the Twelve Gates of the Great City, Jerusalem, a symbol of Man, which are the names of the Twelve Tribes of the Children of Israel; on the east three gates; on the north three gates; on south three gates; and on the west three gates (Gen. 49; Rev. 21:10-13,25).

We have observed that in an extemporaneous statement in the Bible, the God of the Hebrews gave Himself a new name, consisting of the Sacred Four Letters, the mysterious WORD. As it was forbidden for the Jews to pronounce it, it was called the Ineffable Name.

The basic reason for this prohibiting was for the purpose of concealing from the profane and exoteric the fact that the WORD (Ineffable Name) indicated the Four Principle Elements of Creation, symbolized by the Sphinx and which constituted the basis of the Kabala, according to which the first letter, called Yod, expressed the active principle (initiative), the second, called He, the passive principle (receptive), the third, Vau, equilibrium, form, also a link or bridge that united the two; and this union produced the next or second He.

The Kabalists assert that all phenomena and all objects consist of these Four Principles; and so, a study of the WORD and the finding of it in everything, constituted the chief goal of Kabalistic philosophy.

The Ineffable Name was the WORD that was with God, and was God. The Kabalist said, "By a paradox that defies the reasoning faculties, but which is readily resolved intuitively in the Mind, God is apart from, and independent of the Universe, and yet permeates every atom of it."

By discovering the Four Elements in all objects and phenomena of quite different categories, between which the man of darkness sees nothing in common, as the relationship between a man and a tree, the enlightened Initiate sees the analogy between all things, and understands that everything is created and constituted according to the same law and same plan.

The concept is clear and definite; If the WORD, the Ineffable Name, the Four Elements, are in everything, then everything is analogous to the whole, the atom analogous to the Universe, Man analogous to the Creator, and all analogous to the Ineffable Name, J H V H, the WORD which was in the beginning, the WORD which was with God, and the WORD which is God.

And so, a study of the Law of the Four Letters constituted the direct means of discovering the mysteries of Creation, thus improving one's knowledge and of increasing one's Conciousness.

The fact that all living creatures have a Common Ancestor is all that Charles Darwin discovered in his remarkable researches, and that secret of Creation was taught by the Masters for thousands of years before Darwin was ever born.

This is the gospel referred to in the Bible "which ye have heard, and which was preached to every creature which is under heaven;whereof I Paul am made a minister" (Colossians 1:23).

The mind of man has never struggled harder to understand and explain to itself the mystery of Creation and of Divine Manifestation, and at the same time to conceal the discoveries from all but those entitled to receive the knowledge, than the Ancient Masters. Hence, much of their symbology and terminology seems like jargon to all but the Initiated.

The Kabala is the ancient tradition, and its entirety rests on the single dogma of Magism, "The visible is for us the proportional measure of the invisible."

The same doctrine appears in the Bible in these words: "For the invisible things of Him from the creation of the world are clearly seen (in the mind), being understood by the things that are made (visible), even His eternal power and Godhead" (Romans 1:20).

The Masters, observing that equilibrium is the universal law in physics, and that it results from apparent opposition of two forces, positive and passive, they concluded from the physical to the metaphysical equilibrium, and considered that in the Fiery God two properties, necessary to each other, should be recognized.

The principle of equilibrium among all the impersonations, of the male on one side and female on the other to produce balance, is, according to the Kabala , the foundation of all religion and all science.

The
Tarot

"The Tarot is the most ancient of (all) books," wrote Dr. F.H. Curtiss in The Key To The Universe, and he added:

"It is a collection of cards embodying the Secret Doctrine of the ages, almost every (ancient) nation having its version or variation of this synthetic exposition of the Ancient Wisdom.....

"In many respects it is the Key which will unlock the mythical doctrines and philosophies of the Ancient World, and is called the Arcana of the Clavicles of Solomon.

"It is symbolized by a Key whose head is a ring composed of a circle containing the Four Cardinal Signs (of the Zodiakos), the Lion, the Bull, the Eagle and the Angel; its trunk or body bearing the 22 characters , and having the three degrees of the Triad for its wards. It is sometimes called 'The Key of things kept secret from the foundation of the world.'"

The Tarot was lost for centuries, and then suddenly appeared in the 13th century A.D. It originally consisted of four suits of 14 cards each, and there were 22 Trumps Major, making 78 cards in all. This was the source of our deck of ordinary playing cards.

The term Tarot is applied now only to the 22 Major Arcana, and it is evident that the compilers of the Bible had possession of these 22 cards since they included in the Bible much of their symbolism.

Card No. 4 of the Major Arcana is titled The Emperor, and presents the picture of an imposing man seated on a cubic stone, on one side of which is carved an Eagle with outstretched wings, indicative of Animalistic Creation uplifted, or Scorpio transformed; on the other side of the stone is carved a Ram's head, the first sign of the Zodiakos, Aries, a fiery, cardinal sign, in which the Sun is exalted, or raised to its highest level of power. In his right hand the Emperor holds a scepter, signifying Power and Authority. Ouspensky makes him speak, and this is what he wrote:

"I saw the Emperor on his high Throne, decorated with an Eagle and the head of a Ram. A golden helmet gleamed on his brow, and his long white beard fell over his purple mantle. In one hand he held a globe, symbol of the earth, and in the other a Scepter in the form of the Egyptian Cross, the symbol of his power over his creations.

"'I am the Great Law,' said the Emperor. 'I am the Ineffable Name, J H V H. The Four Letters of the Name are in Me, and I am in everything. I am in the Four Principles; I am in the Four Elements; I am in the Four Quarters of the Earth. I am in the Four Signs of the Tarot. I am action; I am resistance; I am completion; I am result. For him who knows the way to see Me, there are no mysteries.

"'As the Earth consists of Fire, Air and Water, and as the Fourth Letter of the Ineffable Name contains the First Three and itself becomes the First, so My Scepter contains the complete Triangel and bears in itself the Seed of a new Triangle.'

"While the Emperor was speaking, His Helmet and the Golden Ar-
mour visible beneath His mantle, shone ever more brightly, until I
could no longer bear the radiance and dropped my eyes. And when I
tried to raise my eyes again, before me there was an all-pervading
Radiance, and Light and Fire. And I fell prostrate worshipping the
Fiery Word, the Living Fire."

We have quoted from Ouspensky the WORDS of the Actor who played
the part of the Emperor in the Ritual of Initiation in the Ancient
Mysteries. This was the source from which the compilers of the Bible
took their material for the first chapter of Genesis.

This is the Great Mystery of the WORD OF GOD, the Tetragrammation. This is the explanation of the reason why the Bible came to
be called the WORD OF GOD.

This chapter should have been titled The Creative Elements, but
we pursued the course of the Masters in confusing the exoteric by
the use of words and symbols, and titled in The Sacred Word: The
Logos of Philo Judaeus and the Demiurge of the Gnostics were scriptures designed to mislead the profane and the impious. That was the
regular trick of the Masters.

Chapter No. 9

ANCIENT MAGIC

The Ancient Masters called their Science by the term of Magic, and we shall see that the term is reasonable and logical.

The Book of Thoth is the most ancient of all books. That strange document has descended to us as a pack of ordinary playing cards. It is a collection of cards constaining a strange symbolism that means little to the masses and yet it conceals the Secret Doctrine of the Ages, almost every nation of antiquity having its version of this synthetic exposition of the Ancient Wisdom.

The Egyptian version was called the Book of Hermes, and the Hebraic, the Book of Adam. In its esoteric aspect, it is the Master Key that unlocks the Secret Doctrines and Mystical Philosophies of the Ancient Masters who invented the symbolism, and it came to be called the Arcana of the Clavicle of Solomon in the Hebraic World.

It was symbolized by a Key whose head was a Ring composed of a Circle containing the Four Cardinal Signs of the Zodiakos, viz., the Lion, the Eagle, the Angel and the Bull. Its stem and body bore the 22 characters of the Hebraic Alphabet, with the three degrees of the Triad for its wards. It was sometimes called "The Key of things kept secret from the foundation of the world."

The original Book of Thoth contained 78 picture cards, but now only the 22 Major Arcana are regarded as symbolizing the Sacred Wisdom, and they are termed the Tarot, a word which literally means a Wheel or an object that rotates, in harmony with the whirling motion of the Earth and all Celestial Bodies.

The Masters understood the Secret of the Cosmic Cycle. In the Jarvis Letters it is said:

"The importance of the picture of the Crb which represented all Wheels, including the Zodiakos, is further shown in the fact that human language was shaped on this Globe, Circle, Wheel. Thus, ORB-IT means 'the motion of the Orb', and even the Rut in the road made by the Wheel is called an 'Orbita' because the Rut reveals the route, rute, ruis or way, or the Road of the Wheel."

-68-

The Magician

Card No. 1 of the Ancient Tarot is titled The Magician. This is
an appropriate symbol of Creative Action.

The Magician appears as a young man, clad in a Magician's robe,
having the countenance of Divine Apollo, with a look of confidence
and brilliant eyes. The sky-colored hat is symbolic of the celestial
world. The lemniscate formed by its brim represents the Cosmic Cycle,
forming the figure 8 lying on its side. About his waist is a serpent-
cincture, the serpent appearing to devour its tail. This is the conventional symbol of Eternity, but here it signifies more especially
the Eternity of Attainment of the Ego or Entity.

In the Magician's left-hand is the Magic Wand, the Caduceus,
the serpent-wound staff of Hermes, pointing toward the sky, thus
indicating the nature of that magical power called Polarity, by
which all Creation occurs. His right-hand points down to the Earth,
ever to remind us that the Terrestrial World is a Reflection of the
Celestial World, according to the ancient aphorism, "As above, so
below."

The Magician stands behind a square table, symbolical of the four hypothetical corners of the Earth. On the table appear four objects which represent the Four Elements of which the Universe is constituted, symbolized by the Sphinx in all nations of antiquity, and indicated by the Four Letters of the Ineffable Name, J H V H, which, in turn, represent Fire, Air, Water and Earth, the fourfold elemental basis of the Universe which appears on each level of Creation in a different guise, and all of them in the ultimate being the congealed essence of Incandescent Gas.

In a deck of common playing-cards the Four Symbols appear as Clubs, Hearts, Diamonds and Spades. By the Masters they were known as the Wand or Scepter, the Cup, the Pentacle, and the Sword. The two colors, red and black, represent the dual aspects of Polarity.

Creation is the Supreme Magic. The great mysteries of the Universe which science can not analyze nor expound, are the regular creative processes constantly occurring all around us, yet so trite and common that we seldom note or reflect upon them.

As an example of Creative Magic, take two small seeds, much alike, and let the chemist decompose them, analyze them, torture them in all the scientific ways at his command. The net result of each seed is some sugar, some fibrin, some water--carbon, potassium, sodium, etc., --one cares not to know what, for to know can tell one nothing.

We plant the two seeds in the soil, which is moistened by the rain and warmed by the sun, and the magical effect of this condition is to activate a mysterious germ in the seed which sends tender shoots up thru the soil and grow as if by magic. And then more magic happens right before our eyes: One shoot develops into a pretty flower, and the other becomes a sturdy bush, of woody fiber, armed with thorns. A miracle that the greatest scientist can neither duplicate nor explain.

This is the creative order of the Four Elements, represented by J H V H. From the earth, the air, the water, under the influence of solar-fire, the mysterious germ in the seed has been activated and it performs its magical work, even producing colors--shades of green that stain the leaves which appear, and then the flowers of many colors and odors.

Creative Magic. Is it any greater miracle to make Man? And so, quite logically, Magic was the ancient name of Science; and very appropriately the title of the first Tarot Card was The Magician.

In their Ritual of Initiation employed to teach the Neophyte
the magic of Creative Action, the Masters used the Circle with the
Dot in its center. The Circle may be expanded to infinity and indicates continuity of space and perpetuity of time. Without beginning and without ending, it signifies the realm of the unmanifested
Zodiakos.

The Circle encompasses all, yet it is the deep Silence of Quies-
cent Equilibrium, the Magical Realm of Invisible Mystery from which,
by transition, there emanates all of that illusory panorama called
the Visible World, called Nature, from Nasci, meaning to be born.

Before any Creative Action occurs, no Law appears. Law, per se,
does not exist. It is not indicated until Equilibrium has been disturbed. This is Creative Action, and the regular, orderly, constant,
changeless mode of motion reveals the Law of Action.

The Dot in the center of the Circle symbolizes the Sun, and
represents the Creative Agent of Creation. The Sun, says the Bible,
"is a bridegroom" coming out of the chamber of God (Ps. 19:5).

In the Egyptian Mysteries, the Sun, in the drama of Initiation,
was personified as Ra for the edification of the Neophyte, and, in
the Ceremony of Initiation, the Actor who personified Ra, spoke and
said:

"I am Ra (Sun) at his first appearance (in the morning). I am
the Great Sun of God......who risest up in thine orb and shinest from
thine Throne.....I come to do the will of the Father, our of the abode
of Flame."

This impressive picture in the chamber of the Great Pyramid, with
glaring lights to add glory to the scene, dramatically arranged,
with the solemn ceremony for the occasion, and able Actors to play
the role of the Creative Forces, formed its impressive part in the
Mystic Drama, staged by the Masters to teach the common Man of Darkness the Magic of Creation. Sadly needed now is such a school.

Polarity

The Circle, in its whirling motion, generates an axis, the verticle line (figure 1), which bisects the Circle into two halves.

No other figure could be the first in the numerical system;
for 1, like the Circle, is a natural geometrical symbol, and the
first figure naturally formed by the first action of Creation.

In the Ancient Mysteries the Neophyte was taught that the primary action of Creative Action is the division of the Circle into equal parts, one negative and one positive. Then Law appears, for Equilibrium has been disturbed as Creative Action begins. This indicates that Law is neither an element nor an entity, but a rule that describes action. Man makes laws by legislative action, but Creation makes laws by Creative Action.

The bisection of the Unit creates Duality, the primary product of Creative Action. The birth of Dualism activates the previously dormant power called Polarity, which now appears as the result of the natural conduct of the Two Halves as they struggle to reunite and reform the original Unit. This makes Polarity one of the most potent and universal of all Laws, described in the dictionary as follows:

The inherent disposition of a body or an elementary molecule, to place its mathematical axis in a particular direction; the disposition of propensity of a body to exhibit opposite or contrasted properties or powers in opposite or contrasted directions; specifically, the existence of two points, called poles, possessing contrary tendencies, as attraction (centripetal) and repulsion (centrifugal) at the opposite ends of the magnet.

Prof. Einstein said, "The Principle of Attraction (Polarity) is the Basic Principle (of Creation) of the Universe, and inherent by nature in every living organism."

F. Huntley wrote: "There is in Nature a universal principle (Polarity) which impels every (particle and every) entity to seek vibratory correspondence with other (particles and) entities of its kind" (Harmonics of Evolution).

J. C. Street, A.B.N., declared: "Polarity is involution and evolution. There can be no evolution without involution. In all the manifestations of Force and Matter, there is but the one Great Law-- Polarity."

The dual process of Involution and Evolution is symbolized in the emblem of the Masters called the Interlaced Triangles, indicating that the Terrestrial World is a Reflection of the Celestial World.

We witness Polarity manifested in repulsive (centrifugal) and attractive (centripetal) action. In the atomic world it is present as the electron and proton; in the chemical it appears as acid and alkaline; in the biological world as male and female; in the mechanical as expansion and contraction.

-72-

It is practically impossible for those who are guided by sight alone, to realize that the different names refer to different phases of One Law and One Action, as all objects and bodies of the visible world are but the numberless variations of One Substance and.One Force. And never forget that all of the various symptoms exhibited by the sick man spring from but One Unitary Cause at the Center, and require but one mode of treatment and care.

And furthermore, the diversity is just a condition of degrees, not of differences. For there is but one force, one substance, one action, one life, one consciousness, one mind, one intelligence, all expressive of infinite activity in a multiplicity of ways, thru a variety of forms.

It is both surprising and edifying to observe the position of our boasted science on the subject of the Universe. The great Dr. Alexis Carrel expressed that opinion of science on this vital point as follows:

"Everyone is aware....that the world is composed of blind and unknown forces; that we are nothing but infinitely small particles on the surface of a grain of dust, lost in the immensity of the cosmos, and that this cosmos is totally deprived of Life and Consciousness. Our Universe is exclusively mechanical. It cannot be otherwise, since it has been created from an unknown substratum by the techniques of physics and chemistry" (Man The Unknown, 1935, p.16).

That blind stupidity is called modern science. We witness the work of Life and Consciousness on all sides of us, yet close our eyes to these facts and deny their existence.

When the curtain fell on Ancient Science in the 4th Century A.D., the Roman Empire plunged head-long into mental darkness, which ruled until the 19th century, that Wonderful Century when Evolutionism was born, and which we have noticed in a preceding chapter.

Think of that thousand years of darkness now being termed the Middle Ages in a world that has existed for billions of years.

Recent discoveries which show the Universe is not "composed of blind and unknown forces" have produced such terms as Divine Law, Natural Law, Cosmic Law, Universal Law, etc., and this Drummond called "the last and most magnificent discovery of Science." But all that science discovered was just its own errors.

And here we encounter another error which science may some day discover. Medical art slyly indicates that the universal laws which

-73-

science has discovered apply not to Man, nor to the condition of his body, which is still subject to the devilish whims of these "blind and unknown forces." His mode of living and his environment have no effect on nor relation to his mental and physical state. His disorder are the result of mysterious germs and viruses, over which he has little or no control, and which attack him when they are ready or have a chance.

Science has at last discovered that Creative Processes are in constant operation everywhere, always in the same direction, in a definite manner, without variation or change, which knowledge enables us to predict with exactitude that a thousand years hence, grass will grow and water run as at this present moment.

If this newer knowledge were systematically applied to the human body and rigidly observed, the results would be astounding. Sickness would disappear, doctors would have little to do, Medical Art would vanish and become a sad memory, and the human life-span would soon double and triple. This startling fact is known to a few leading lights of the Medical World, but they are forced into silence for the sake of their profession.

It is the general belief that Sir Isaac Newton discovered what is known as the Law of Gravitation. He presumed he had discovered the operation of some unknown force which he called Gravity because he could think of no better name. To him, the force now called electro-magnetism was unknown. He had never heard of it, and knew not that the Earth floats in a gigantic electro-magnetic sea that has a pressure, at sea-level, of a little more than two thousand pounds a square foot. What he did discover was the polaristic properties of repulsion and attraction of this then unknown sea. That was his Gravity.

The Law of Gravitation speaks to science only of processes. It has no data to offer as to itself. The Law predicates nothing of causation, but only of effects, and these effects are what Newton discovered.

In every field of activity, Law indicates that effects are the result of causes, and that we reap as we sow (Gal. 6:7). If this knowledge were properly taught in the schools, we would know that we must suffer in direct ratio with the degree of our transgressions that violate the eternal rule as to the requirements of our body.

Give the body the care it should lawfully have, and human ailments will vanish and become unknown, as in the case of bugs and birds. That high state of the body is not gained by vaccination and

-74-

inoculation, nor by a study of the body's derangements, but by learning the body's needs and requirements, and supplying them.

The Trinity

The Doctrine of the Trinity is one of the most mysterious and most misunderstood of all religious dogmas. It can be comprehended only by going back to the Ancient Wisdom and determining its basic meaning.

The Ancient Wisdom was based on facts not fallacies. It dealt with Creation. Worlds and planets are created bodies of the highest type, and, for their creation, Cosmic Consciousness requires power proportionate to the gigantic task. And modern science holds "that this cosmos is totally deprived of Life and Consciousness."

Our schools neither know nor teach what they should--that Creation represents the action and product of terrific and violent force. Let us consider an intermediary stage thereof--blazing Sun, for instance. Here is a case of Creative Consciousness making a universal body, and where are the moral qualities? God is Love says the blind religionist.

The Sun, is a terrible, non-moral body, so fierce that were it not for the protective atmosphere of the Earth, it would destroy us a hundred million miles away. And the Creative Cause of Action is within it. That Cause is the Creator, ruthless and destructive.

He who thinks this is contrary to the Bible, does not know the Bible. God is called therein a Consuming Fire; and what is more terrible than a roaring Fire out of control? Also the first name by which He was known to the Hebrews is El Shaddai, which means "terrible power," "that which treats with violence," etc., Nor were they alone in thus considering the Creator. Ages before, the Hindus called God Jagannath--"ruthless power."

This terrific Creative Power is potent power derived from the latent and incalculable source we call space, and it must be organized and intelligized by Cosmic Consciousness. And so, (1) Cosmic Consciousness, (2) Creative Power, and (3) Created Products (Planets, suns, etc.), form the first and original Trinity of Being.

The first two are Causes, the third is Effect. The first two are mutually interdependent; that is, neither Cosmic Consciousness alone nor Creative Power alone, can accomplish Creative Action.

Cosmic Consciousness must be fortified with Creative Power, and the latter must be organized and intelligized by Cosmic Consciousness. And so, the two are inextricably united throughout the entire Creative Process, thus forming the dual aspect of the Divine Trinity. The product of their united action is the Effect which forms the third aspect and completes the Primal Trinity of the Ancient Wisdom.

The High Priestess

The Masters symbolized this phase of Creative Action in Card 2 of the Ancient Tarot, titled the High Priestess, who symbolized the World Mother. At her feet is the lunar crescent, a horned diadem is on her head, with a globe between the horns, and a solar cross on her breast.

In her lap there lies a Scroll, on which is inscribed the word Tora, the phoenic equivalent of the Hebraic Torah, the Law. It is partly concealed by her mantle, to signify that certain phases of Creation can be discerned by the physical senses, the exoteric part. The esoteric, or hidden part, must be apprehended by the application of an open, unprejudiced Mind.

Reason, divorced from Cosmic Consciousness, can discern only the realm of effects, the illusionary world in which science works and seldom sees what it thinks it sees. United with Cosmic Consciousness, which science claims does not exist, reason can penetrate the obscuring mantle which conceals Creation's most secret pages, and pursue its mysteries to their finality.

The High Priestess is seated before and between two Pillars, the Masonic Jachin and Boaz of Solomon's Temple. They signify the Positive and Negative properties of Polarity, and, by the Masters, were termed the World Father (Positive) and the World Mother (Negative). Behind her, extending between the Pillars is a Veil which conceals from view the Mysteries of Creation, and it is not to be rudely lifted by the profane nor desecrated by the impious.

The Universal Polar Powers inherent in the World Father and the World Mother are forever pulling them together in the constant attempt to reform the original Unit and restore Cosmic Equilibrium. That course activates the Secondary Phase of Creation, and Procreation results as the effect.

This was the fable invented by the Ancient Masters and dramatized in the Ancient Mysteries to teach the Neophyte the magic and mystery of Creation.

This is the basic interpretation of the Ancient Doctrine of the
Trinity. In the Ancient Philosophy it appeared as the World Father,
the World Mother, and the World Son--a very old doctrine which long
ago lost its original meaning in the hands of the priesthood and used
by them to exalt themselves and enslave the masses.

Dr. F. H. Curtiss mentioned the Doctrine in his Key To The
Universe, and believed it referred to a "three-fold Deity," He wrote:

"Number 3 is sacred and divine because it symbolizes the three-
fold Deity, the Trinity: the Father, the Mother, and the Son; the
Brahma, Vishnu, and Siva of the Hindus; the Osiris, Isis, and Horus
of the Egyptians" (p. 102).

Curtiss thought it better not to go on and mention more cases
of the Trinity, including Oromasdes, Mithras, and Ahriman of the
Persians; Odin, Thor, and Frey of the Scandinavians; God, Mary and
Jesus of the Christians, etc. We must withhold some of the facts if
we would not be anathematized and excommunicated by the Church.

In the ancient scriptures of the Chinese it is written:"The
Source and Root of all is One. This self-existent Unity necessarily
produced a second, and the first and the second, by their union,
produced a third. These Three produced all" (Doane, Bible Myths,
p. 372).

We observe that the Ancient Doctrine of the Trinity did not mean
three gods in one. It meant the Trio of Original Entities that were
created by the Primary Creative Action. In the fable, two of them
were produced by the bisection of the Cosmic Unit, and the third
came into being from the natural propensity of the Two Halves to reunite and reform the Original Unit. In what other way could the
story be better told?

To summarize: The Primary Act of Creation bisects the Circle
into Two Halves. Then polarity appears as the Power that pulls the
Two Halves back together to reform the Original Unit, with Procreation resulting as the Effect.

This was the ancient hypothesis of the origin of the Trinity,
consisting of what was called the World Father, the World Mother, and
the World Son, who became the Savior of the world under the clever
manipulations of the cunning priesthood. It was only a postulate invented by the Masters to present the supernal nature of Creative
Action in concrete terms of the Human Seeding Group, the Holy Family.

Secondary Creation

When the hidden meaning of the Ancient Philosophy is known and explained, mystery vanishes and wonder increases as to the marvels of the human body. We are now going to understand the Principle of Sexuality, which has been such a puzzle to science, and still is.

Modern science has never yet discovered that there are two phases of Creative Action:

(1) The Primary Phase which produces bodies and organisms, and (2) the Secondary Phase which perpetuates the products of the Primary Phase.

Created organisms come into being fully endowed with the power by which they are competent to perpetuate themselves. This secondary creation is termed Procreation, and it is properly the Secondary Phase of Creation.

In this phase of Creative Action the great scientists have discovered nothing more than what they consider to be a condition forced upon humanity by a gross physical passion, regarded by the great evolutionist, Charles Darwin, as a "mania," and condemned in the Bible as Carnal Lust.

According to Darwinism, Sexuality has no other purpose than that of physical propagation, which is entirely in the interest of the species. When Darwin had thus considered the subject, he was done with it. Anything more or higher in the form of spiritual, astral, vital, intellectual or moral improvement of man was utterly unthinkable.

The Superstitous Heathens of antiquity were broader minded and better biologists. They believed that great possibilities for the body were also inherent in the Secondary Phase of Creation, and would greatly benefit the body in many ways if procreation were inhibited, controlled or curtailed.

The Superstitious Heathens knew that cosmic processes are usually dual in action and effect, presenting both a constructive and a destructive aspect. They saw the dual action presented in the power of the Sun. It not only generates but also degenerates. Why not a similar duality apply to the Secondary Phase of Creation in the case of Man?

This thought constrained the Masters to apply assiduous attention to the body's procreative function; and for so doing they have been well smeared with the epithet Sex Worshippers. And so they were, but for a very high and grand purpose. Their discovereis were so amazing that they have been guarded with great secrecy, being imparted only to the Neophyte, under oath, in the Ancient Mysteries.

This phase of our subject is so important and means so much in the higher development of man, that we have devoted another work to it, dealing largely with the Mindand its processes.

Chapter No. 10

Creative Cycle

As hard as humanity works and searches for knowledge, and as so much time and money are expended in research for knowledge, it is difficult to believe that entire libraries have been burned to destroy knowledge. But such are the bald facts of history, and that information is now called "hate literature" when published and passed on to the brainwashed slaves of modern times.

Science admits that it can tell us little about Life on this whirling globe, and less about its origin, its purpose, and its ultimate fate. But such fragments of the scriptures of the Superstitious Heathens as have escaped the hand of destruction, disclose the fact to him who is competent to interpret their clever symbols and fables, that these Ancient Heathens were far ahead of us in knowledge relating to the Riddle of Life and the Mystery of Creation.

Those Ancient Heathens discovered that there is a Creative Cycle which has no beginning and no ending, the course of which runs as regular and certain as the rising and setting of the sun. They called it the Wheel of Life, and symbolized it in their Zodiakos and their Tarot Card No. 10, presented here. But practically all data concerning this symbolism have been lost or destroyed, and we are warned in dictionaries, histories and encyclopedias that the Zodiakos was the stupid work of Superstitious Heathens; that everything related in it and to it was foolish, deceptive, and should be discountenanced.

10. Wheel of Life

We have discovered enough in our seventy long years of experience and researching for knowledge to be constrained to believe,
that the Ancient Masters and their Zodiakos were far from being what
we have been told they are. We have found enough to indicate to us
that these Heathens were scientists of the first order, and that
their symbolism, including their Zodiakos and their Tarot Cards, concealed an amazing story relative to the Creative Cycle. Some of
that story we shall proceed to describe.

The greatest mysteries in the Universe are those which are ever
going on all around us; so trite and common to us that we never note
them or reflect upon them. Some phases of the Creative Cycle are
simple and understood, but other phases are more complex and mysterious. It is the latter which we shall consider, and much that we
shall reveal will surprise the reader.

It is in order to begin with the Glorious Sun, without which
the earth would soon become as barren as a cobble stone. In all ages
the Sun has been recognized as the source of physical light, warmth
and virility of our little planet, and thus naturally has been closely connected with the ancient philosophy of the Creator as FIRE.

All the Celestial Bodies were regarded as manifested centers of
Celestial Fire of the Cosmos, the source of which was said to be the
Invisible Sun, termed the Sun behind the Sun.

The Sun is so far away that it can never be reached. One cannot even look at it when it is at its zenith. It is impossible to
visualize its full effect upon the earth, or to observe its generative quality in the concrete.

The Sun is a terrible, non-moral body, so fierce that were it.
not for the protective atmosphere of the earth, it would destroy us
a hundred million miles away. Yet the creative cause is within it,
not without, and that cause is the Creator, being not a God of Love
but of ruthless and destructive power.

He who thinks this is contrary to the Bible doesn't know the
Bible. God is called therein a Consuming Fire (Deut. 4:24; Heb. 12:
29, etc.); and what is more terrible than a roaring Fire out of Control? Also, the first and regular name by which He was known to the
Hebrews was El Shaddai, which means "terrible power," "that which
treats with violence," etc. Nor were they the only people thus to
consider the Creator. Ages before, the Hindus called God Jagannath
--"ruthless power."

The Sun is the heart and center of our Universe. Its work is
directed and regulated by the Creative Intelligence contained in its

Essence. Its Flaming Radiance presents three phases: (1) The Spirit of the Flame, (2) the Light of the Flame, and (3) the Heat of the Flame.

When we consider the Radiant Flame, we gain a clearer conception of the Trinal Nature of the Creator, or the Primordial Trinity, the three phases manifested by Creative Power.

Like the Heart of the Microcosm (Man), the Solar Heart of the Macrocosm (Universe) governs the radiation and circulation of the Animative Essence throughout the entire Solar System, comparable to the blood of the human body; and at every return of the Animative Essence to the Solar Heart, it contracts regularly in a rhythmic cadence, comparable to the function of the human heart. But instead of the rhythmic beats occurring in approximately a second of time, as they do in the heart of man, it requires a period of ten years for the Solar Fluid of electrical substance to circulate thru the entire system, and another year, making a total of ELEVEN, for it to pass thru the auricle and ventricle, be purified by the Great Breath, and be prepared and made ready to pass out again thru the arteries of the Universe.

This Creative Cycle of Eleven Years is well-known to astronomers, but they are ignorant of its correspondence with the functions of the human body. During that period, the sun-spots regularly increase numerically and in intensity.

For data on the subject, the ancient Chinese and Egyptian records were studied as far back as 220 B.C., to help determine sun-spot and aurora borealis activity; and the records showed that there have been changes in this Cycle for sun-spot activity. The serious famines and droughts recorded in Asia reflect the effect of the Solar Cycle.

If the human heart were made luminous and the throbbing organ made visible, so as to have it reflected on a screen, then we would see the sun-spot phenomena reflected every second.

Just as the Great Electrified Breath of the Universe moves the planets in space and regular order, so that same power, entering the human body, moves the mystery Entity in it from one experience to another, from one physical form to another, and even from one world to another, as in the case when this earth terminates in a terrific explosion as stated in chapter 7.

This refers to the Celestial Body mentioned in the Bible (1 Cor. 15:40), and is the Creative Cycle of Reincarnation, mentioned in the Bhagavad-Gita in these words; "Both thou and I have passed thru many births."

Astronomers are aware of the fact that every Eleven Years the
Earth passes thru an especially dense stream of meteors, proving
that the Earth receives a special influx of physical substance every
Eleven Years from other systems in space, which supplies the Earth
with material needed for the New Cycle of Action.

The Ten Year Period required for the Solar Substance to circulate
thru the entire Universal System was symbolized by the Ancient
Heathens in the 10th card of the Tarot as stated, which depicts a
Circle called the Wheel of Life.

These wise Masters understood the fact that the Macrocosm and
the Microcosm correspond to one uniform, mathematical law that rules
everything from plant to planet, from angle-worm to angel divine,
from man to mouse, from the vegetation which carpets the earth to
the stars which stud the sky.

Our great work is to get out of the darkness of modern science
and learn to relate and relatize the sensible products of Creation
to their occult analogy, as the Masters did. Then we will discover,
in constant operation everywhere, the Creative Force of the Macrocosm.

The Wheel of Life portrayed in Tarot Card No. 10, is pivoted
upon the upper end of the verticle 1, and at its base are entwined
the two Serpents of the Caduceus, which symbolize the dual aspects
of Polarity.

Poised with outspread wings above the top of the Wheel is the
Sphinx, the Great Symbol of the Sacred Four Elements of Creation,
mentioned in Chapter 8. On the right side of the Wheel, ascending,
is Anubis, the Egyptian symbol of Good, bearing in its right paw the
Magic Wand. On the left side of the Wheel, descending, is Typhon,
the Egyptian symbol of Evil. These two figures indicate the doctrine that Good is the uplifting force, while Evil is ever fleeing
from it and descending into darkness and disintegration.

The balanced position of the Sphinx in the picture, signifies
the command and supremacy that Wisdom exercises over Good and Evil.
Anubis and Typhon represent the opposition of these qualities, and
indicate that Evil must disintegrate so that its Force may revert
and manifest as Good in the next upward movement of the Wheel of Life.

Every No. 10 indicates a return to Unity, and at return there
is brought new experience that promotes improvement. This is expressed by the digit which is a manifestation of the 10.

As the 10 continues to recur in its multiples, each 10 symbolizing the Creative Cycle of progressive evolution and experience, likewise the Fiery God, or the Eternal Ego in the terrestrial Temple adds experience to experience throughout the Creative Cycle, in its long journey to Individualization and Perfectionization.

And just as each time a 10 is reached, its value is raised by the power of the new digit (20,30,40, etc.), and its greater Cycles are indicated by the additions of the Circles (1000,1000,100000,etc.) so does the Ego add to its experience as it passes thru its minor incarnations on the earth plane, each dominated by a special phase of development comparable to an added digit.

Then, at a certain cyclic periods, the Ego reaches decisive or major incarnations in which, like No. 10, it adds to itself the continuity of its great and original mission of manifestation.

Obviously, this is a newer and higher Cycle, during which the Ego develops or adds to its experiences, the great and higher powers of manifestation, just as the number 1 adds more circles. Each new Circle means that the Ego has passed on to a new and, as yet, unmanifested experience, a higher phase of experience than those it has expressed and passed.

One of the numerous allegories in the Bible refers to these experiences of the Ego, the Fiery God that dwells in the terrestrial Temple, showing that this phase of the Creative Cycle was known to and recognized by the Ancient Masters. In verses 9-12, Chapter 7 of Revelation, it is written:

"After this I beheld, and, lo, a great multitude, which no man could number, of all nations, and kindreds, and people, and tongues, stood before the throne,and before the Lamb, clothed in white robes, and palms in their hands; and cried with a loud voice, saying, Salvation to our God who sitteth upon the throne (of Life), and unto the Lamb (Ego).

"And all the angels stood round about the throne, and about the elders, and the four beasts, and fell down before the throne on their faces, and worshipped the (Fiery) God, saying, Amen: Blessing, and glory, and wisdom, and thanksgiving, and honor, and power, and might, be unto our God (the Ego) forever and ever, Amen."

Very baffling and mysterious. Now for the simple interpretation of the fable: The great multitude, clothed in white robes, represents the billions of atoms (creative elements) which constitute the terrestrial body of man, and these are liberated from the human

form by its disintegration after the Fiery God has departed there-
from in the creative process called Death, a regular and orderly
occurrence that is so terrifying to those who follow science and
live in darkness.

The Lamb represents the Animative Element of the Body called
Life, the Ego, the Fiery God. The angels represents the millions
of Celestial Egos that have been liberated by Death from their
terrestrial bodies. The elders represent the twelve signs of the
Zodiakos, and the Four Beasts are the four animals that constitute
the Sphinx.

Same chapter of Revelation, verses 13-17:-

"And one of the elders (in the fable) answered, saying unto me,
What are these which are arrayed in white robes? and whence came
they? And I said unto him, Sir, thou knowest. And he said to me,
These are they which came out of great tribulation (from the human
body), and have washed their robes, and made them white in the blood
of the Lamb. Therefore are they before the throne of the God, and
serve him day and night in his temple; and he that sitteth on the
throne shall dwell among them. They shall hunger no more, neither
thirst any more; neither shall the sun light on them, nor any heat.
For the Lamb which is in the midst of the throne (of Life) shall
feed them, and shall lead them unto living fountains of water; and
the God shall wipe away all tears from their eyes."

Interpretation: The great ordeal of the Fiery God, the Ego, is
in its Incarnations in the Terrestrial Body, that it may appear upon
the Earth, not merely for the term of one short life-span, but during a long series of Incarnations throughout the aeons of generations, and not in just one body, but in billions of bodies.

And the Fiery God has its own mighty purpose in thus "crucify-
ing" itself upon the Cross of Life by confining itself in a terrestrial prison on the earth, descending into the spheres of generation
and passing thru vast cycles of Creation. For that is the regular
order of the Infinite Creative Cycle, in constant operation, and
unknown to the Man of Darkness.

Not the human mother, but the Fiery God of the Universe, using
the human mother as its workshop as previously mentioned, builds for
its earthly habitation, out of the creative elementions mentioned
in Chapter 8, a form that fits it for the Terrestrial World, and by
unremitting toil throughout the aeons, it individualizes and per-
fectionizes the Eternal Entity, the Immortal Ego, to that degree of
evolutionary perfection, that future incarnations are not necessary
for that particular Entity, whose work in the Terrestrial World thus
is finished.

And when the creative elements are released unto their natural freedom by the disintegration of the Dead Body of Man, in which "their robes" were literally washed" and made White by the blood of the Lamb", but not the gospel Jesus, they are free of all the body's sensations, such as hunger, and thirst, and breath, and are not affected by sun-light and heat, and shed no tears.

SEPTENNATION

The Ancient Masters were scientific Creationists, not crack-pot Evolutionists. In dealing with Creative Action, they understood and recognized the universal Law of Septennation. They realized that in Creation there are Seven Divisions, Seven Planes and Seven Elements. Evidence of the Septenary Division we find everywhere as we examine Created Phenomena as a whole.

The Bible says, "Wisdom (Creation) hath builded her house; she hath hewn out her Seven Pillars." It mentions Seven Lamps of Fire burning before the throne, the Seven Spirits of God, the Seven Angels, the Seven Vials, the Book with Seven Seals, the Seven Kings, etc. (Pro. 9:1; Rev. 4:5; 5:1; 17:1,10)

There are more than a hundred references to the number 7 in the first three books of the Bible. That is but a fragment of the Ancient Wisdom concerning Creation that has been lost, and scorned by physical science because not understood.

Referring to Cosmic Radiation Phenomena, Hallenbach said, "It has been established from the standpoint of phenomenal law, upon which rests all our knowledge (of Creation), that the vibrations of sound and light increase regularly and divide naturally into seven columns."

There are 7 divisions of the chemical elements, 7 divisions in the electro-magnetic spectrum, 7 tones in the musical scale, and Seven Great Rays constitute the manifested aspect of Creative Action.

The Ancient Masters knew this universal Law of Septennation applies to Life and Man. Then held that in the case of each person, Seven Incarnations are experienced by the Ego, the Fiery God. This law is recognized in the Bible in the case of the Hero of Revelation, who seemed to know that he had passed thru Five Incarnations,--the story being told in these words:

"There are Five Kings (Incarnations); and five (Incarnations) are fallen (gone into oblivion), and one (Incarnation) is (present), and the other Seventh Incarnation) is not yet come; and when he

(Seventh Incarnation) cometh, he must continue for a short space"
(of one life-span) (Rev. 17:10).

Seven signifies the nuptial unition of Spirit and Matter on the
physical plane, and the completion of the first octave of Creation.
Seven (Fourteen) Double indicates the Portal where Man, on the terrestrial plane, must pause, rest, study the path which he has traver-
sed, and accumulate strength to continue his journey.

The ancient Greeks associated the number 14 with the Cycle of
Reincarnation, their doctrine being that the Celestial Body, the Ego,
about to be reborn on earth, drank of the Waters of Lethe ere it
resumed another pilgrimage. By imbibition of the Waters of Lethe,
a fabulous river of the lower world, the Celestial Body happily for-
got its former terrestrial experiences.

This forgetfulness would be undesirable had the previous incarnation been a pleasant life. But such does not occur in the flesh
that is the slave of hate, greed, jealousy, lust of sensation,etc.
And so, it is a perfect state which Creation prepares, that Man may
return to earth in a new body and a mind completely cleansed of its
previous sad experiences from which Death had kindly released him.

Reincarnation

In the case of Man, the Law of the Creative Cycle is logically
the Law of Reincarnation. As stated, the Masters called it the
Wheel of Life and symbolized it in their Tarot Card No. 10, and also
in the Zodiakos.

When we delve deeply, and with understanding, into the meaning
of the ideographs of the Ancient Masters, we discover that the
strange symbolism of the Zodiakos concealed the mystery of Man. The
whole schemata of the Ideogram was for the purpose of demonstrating
and elucidating the relationship existing between the Macrocosm and
the Microcosm, the Creator and the Created.

We should not forget that in all the world there is only one
story told in the Ancient Scriptures, and that is the story of Man.
He is the Key to the Scriptures and to all the Symbolism of the
Masters; and Reincarnation was the Secret Doctrine of the great re-
ligions of antiquity, including Brahamanism, the origin of which extends back so far, that its beginning is lost in the night of time.
Their Scriptures are called the Upanishads, and therein it was written:

"As man, casting off worn-out garments, taketh new ones, so the Dweller in the body, casting off worn-out frames, entereth into others that are new and bright."

In another very ancient Scripture, the Egyptian Book of the Dead, it was said that the Ego, projecting itself into one physical embodiment after another, "steppeth onward through eternity."

The ancient Greeks stated in their Scriptures that the Ego is "more ancient than the body," as it had travelled the Creative Cycle of Incarnation in many bodies, donning and doffing them as vestures of contact with the terrestrial world, so that it might accumulate and store up the knowledge of all Life, garnered by experience in every terrestrial body it had occupied.

In fact, the nature of the relationship of the Celestial and the Terrestrial Bodies in each and every one of its incarnate periods, was not only the nub of the ancient philosophy, but the very core of all biblical meaning.

When the ancient philosophy of Reincarnation was revived in the Western World, the public at large eagerly embraced the Doctrine because it was natural and logical; and now the belief therein is widespread because the late discovereis of science have shattered its own crude materialism and Evolutionism.

Many have failed to observe that the gospel Jesus believed in and espoused the ancient Doctrine of Reincarnation. This is shown by the fact that he asked his disciples, saying, "Whom do men say that I, the Son of Man, am? And they said, Some say thou art John the Baptist; some, Elias; and others, Jeremias, or one of the (reincarnated) prophets" (Mat. 16:13,14).

Origen, the pupil of Flavius Titus Clement of Alexandria, previously mentioned, held the Doctrine of Reincarnation to be Christian. One author says that the purposeful exclusion of this Key Doctrine from Christian counsels and systematism after the denunciation of it by the Second Council of Constantinople in the year 553 A.D has been the chief influence that plunged the Western World, since the fifth century, into a riot of lawlessness unmatched in history. which continues unto this day.

As the matter is of considerable moment from the purely historical standpoint, it is desirable that we give here the very words of the decree by which the Mother Church anathematized and excommunicated the doctrine out of its theology. This datum of church history is an item quite obscure and has been difficult to locate, therefore its inclusion here should be appreciated.

The decree was couched in the following sentence: "Whosoever shall support the mythical doctrine of the pre-existence of the human soul, and the consequent wonderful opinion of its return to earth, let him be anathema."

The occasion and timing of this decree are evidence that the belief in Reincarnation had been more or less deeply ingrained in general Christian doctrinism. The two great heads of the Leading Christian Seminary, the renowned school at Alexandria, which gave the first definite formulation to Christian theology, viz., Clement and Origen, had upheld the doctrine.

Other evidence of its prevalence in Christianity are found. But we can be sure that much of the evidence for it in the Christian movement has been obliterated in that frenzy of destruction with which the pious zealots of the faith swept up and burned all literary vestiges of the ancient antecedents of their rites and doctrines.

In the Ancient Mysteries it was taught that the ordinary period of time between Incarnations is usually 144 years. And so, in the Bible the number of the "sealed" is stated to be 144,000 (Rev. 7:4), the three ciphers being added to mislead the esoteric and confuse the profane.

Numbers

The researches of the great Pythagoras revealed that the Creative Cycle presents a definite regularity that corresponds to numbers. He said "The Universe is formed upon the principle of numbers and the numbers are the Key to an understanding of the mystery of Creative Processes."

Numbers represent facts, not fancies. They typify Creative Action and conceal "the rejected stone not used by the present builders."

The Great Pyramid of Gizeh, erected by the Masters of a distant prehistoric past, presents the lost secret of numbers. Of it one author wrote:

"An extreme precision, an object at which the mind stands truly aghast and confounded, appears to have presided at the operation and goedetic calculations of the Pyramid Builders."

No matter how far back into the night of time investigations are carried, high levels of civilization are found, and each had an elaborate numerical system. Numbers conceal supersensual designs, yet retained in their concealment a spiritual significance. It is a fact that "the infinity of numbers is a state proven to the mind, yet of which no proof can be given of its materiality."

The Hebraic numbers and letters, borrowed by them from their more advanced and enlightened neighbors, hold the Key that unlocks the language of symbolism and universal principles. They were originally traced out like the Constellations, the Masters declaring that Man, the Created Microcosm, must essentially be a Living Reflection of the Creating Macrocosm. And the Bible supports this postulate by stating that God created Man in His Image and Likeness. Therefore, the Masters logically said, "As above, so below."

The first twelve letters and numbers of the Hebrews correspond to the Twelve Zodiakal Constellations, beginning with Taurus, the Bull, and ending with Aries, the Ram. The rest of their 22 letters (double 11) were also an astral alphabet.

Death

The Ancient Masters realized that in Man's primeval, incompleted cycles of incarnation, the demise of the mortal body is a regular process of the Creative Cycle, and is really unrecognized blessing in disguise, the event being dreaded only because not understood, and made worse by being shrouded in darkness designed to intensify the fear.

The general horror of this orderly phase of the Creative Cycle called Death is not natural in the case of Man. For he should be informed all phases of Creative Action are governed by law, and their purpose is progressive improvement. The time is long past due when this terrifying fear of Death should be banished from the Mind of Man by proper teaching as to the basic facts of Creation.

It is the work of scheming trickery that such a blighting, withering, libellous concept was invented and promoted, that in the creative processes of the omnipotent, omniscient Creator, there could be any part of the Creative Cycle that should strike to the human heart such unwarranted horror as that which, for no other reason than fraudulent misrepresentation of the Creator's great work, prevails as the Creative Process called Death of the mortal body.

The story is related in the Bible that Man was driven from the fabulous Garden of Eden for his own good, lest he eat of the Tree of Life and Live forever in a prison of flesh (Gen. 3:22-24).

The Masters who invented that fable based it upon wisdom and science. For they knew that Man must shed his mortal, corruptible garment of the Dust of the Ground, lest it endure forever in its hate, greed, lust and evil, thus holding its Godly Occupant a helpless prisoner in its grip, preventing his liberation from that vile dungeon of corruption, and hindering his lawful progress to a higher estate.

Understanding the mystery of the Creative Cycle, the Masters said in their scriptures, Better is the day of thy Death than the day of thy Birth (Eccl. 7:1).

The Ancient Masters discovered the secret of the Creative Cycle in the simple case of invisible vapor, which condenses to water, then to ice, and returns again as vapor to the invisible world: Not in EXTINCTION BUT IN SUSPENSION, potentially existent, and ready to reappear (reincarnate) in the visible world when the condition for such reappearance (reincarnation) is suitable and favorable.

Every phase of the Creative Cycle in the case of water is perceptible except the one arc in which the water returns to invisible vapor (spirit) and vanishes from sight. That is the point where science gets lost. For, according to materialism, when anything vanishes from sight, that is the end of it; it has gone out of existence.

Due to the erroneous teaching of materialistic science in our schools, the people are so ignorant of the Law of the Creative Cycle that if we should ask a college graduate to analyze some phase of the Cycle, he'd raise his eyebrows in surprise and ask, "What's that? I never heard of it."

Practically nothing of value touching upon Creation is taught in the schools and colleges. What's the reason of that? All questions have answers, and all we must do is desire deeply enough to know this answer, and it will come, provided we have the perception to recognize it. In this particular case, the Desire may be present, but the perception to recognize the answer is, for a definite reason, absent. That reason is the sheer fear of bald facts when they explode theological fancies.

Who wants to part with the gospel Jesus. He was invented to "save lost souls" and he is not needed in the case of Reincarnation. We return and try to do better than we did the time before. And Seven Incarnations polish us off and perfectionize us to the point that we are prepared for the higher plane of Life. That is the work of the Creative Cycle. That was the basic teaching of the Ancient

Philosophy, and also of Christianity until is was anathematized and
excommunicated by the Mother Church.

The various fables relating to immortality in the flesh, such
as The Wandering Jew, etc., were designed to portray the horrific
fate of eternal life in the flesh, which no one would desire if all
the facts were known and considered. Contemplate the endless misery
Man would suffer for ages without end, if he could not shed his decre-
pit, feeble, painful body.

Life is Creation's greatest treasure for Man in the flesh, and
most men should enjoy that priceless treasure much longer than they
do. This can readily be accomplished by learning the body's simple
requirements, and living in harmony with that knowledge. Some men
are living 120, 150, 200 years and even more, and what is possible
in one case is obviously possible in millions of more cases.

In 1916 Goddard E. Diamond died in San Francisco at the age of
120, and we have a letter from a lady dated June 10, 1961, advising
us that she danced with him in San Francisco in 1901 when he was 105
years old.

In 1943 Santiago Surviate, an Indian, died in Arizona at the age
of 134. In 1936 Zora Agha, a Turk, died in Turkey at the age of 162.
In 1921 Jose Calvario died in Mexico at the age of 185. In 1795 Thomas
Carn died in England at the age of 207. In 1933 Li Chung-Yun died
in China at the age of 256. In 1566 Numas De Cugna died in India at
the age of 370. He grew four new sets of teeth and his hair turned
from black to grey four times.

There are just a few of the cases of remarkable longevity which
we have picked from our file. There are many reasons, most of them
preventable, why people die young and why hospitals are filled with
the sick to the roof, whereas others are seldom sick and live from
three to ten times longer.

The basic reason of illness and early death is no mystery. The
condition is governed by the Law of Cause and Effect; and foolish is
he who believed that this law can be nullified, as medical art false-
ly claims, by vaccines, serums, drugs or any other means and methods
employed by doctors.

The Bible says that we reap just as we sow (Gal. 6:7); and the
experience of thousands of years proves the truth of that ancient
axiom, but the fact is usually unnoticed. Even in cases of untimely
death by accident, the contributing cause is generally some sort of
carelessness or recklessness.

The Creative Cycle thru which the Ego passes is portrayed in the Hebraic numbers from 1 to 22, is symbolized in the 22 Trumps Major of the Ancient Tarot, and is graphically allegorized in Bunyan's Pilgrim's Progress.

On that journey, each Rest House might be compared to a number where the Pilgrim, having conquered the dangers thru which he has passed, may rest and refresh himself and receive wise council and more strength for his new beginning. No 11 represents the Pilgrim starting out afresh on his journey of terrestrial life after his first rest period.

The Hebraic number 11 stands for the plural of two, meaning to repeat. The Hebraic word for 11 is Achad, Osher, Ai, or one of ten. God and God. Eliphas Levi connects 11 with Astral Light, which he calls the great Magical Agent in which all things are reflected. He also calls it Manas, or Man's higher and lower Mind. This postulate he based upon the ability of Man's Mind to extend up to the greatest heights or to descend to the lowest depths.

That postulate is correct. For at No. 11 Man receives a new influx of strength and, having free-will, he must decide whether to use it for Good or Evil. If he has not conquered the desires of the flesh, it will be for Evil.

And the two figures, 11, standing side by side, is what Levi called the Magic Chain, asserting that whenever two or more persons stand side by side, united in thoughts and lines of action, they form a magic chain capable of influencing others.

Apollonius, the great Pythagorean philosopher of the First Century, in considering the hours of Initiation in the Ancient Mysteries, makes 10 the first hour. It is an hour of joy; the Neophyte has finished his trial of Initiation and passed its terrible tests. Yet it is also an hour of further trial and much depends upon it.

The ancient Egyptian used the Sphinx as a symbol of the first hour, calling it the Guardian of the Ancient Arcana. The human head of the image, at this stage, says to the Aspirant for the higher cycle, "First acquire knowledge"; its bull's thighs indicate to him, "Be strong and patient in thy work"; its lion's paws says to him, "Thou must be fearless and fight to defend thyself against all evil"; its eagle's wings say, "Thou must will to rise toward the Celestial World which thy Ego already approachest."

No. 11 is the second hour, and Apollonius calls it the "Abyss of fire--the virtues of the Stars close as a Crown thru the Dragons and the fire (the magnetic chain)."

At this point, the Neophyte must learn to distinguish the course of the positive and negative currents of vital force in his body, also to distinguish between Good and Evil, and to choose between them.

As stated, the Tarot consisted of 22 Trumps Major, double 11. The 11th card had two titles, the older one being Strength and the latter being Justice. The older title is more fitting for this occasion. It presents a young woman who, with her hands, opens and closes without effort the powerful jaws of an angry lion. She wears a crown surmounted by a vase and crowned with eagles, and at her brow is the Sacred Serpent.

The base is symbolical of the affections, and the crowned eagles represent the spiritualistic aspect of force. The Serpent indicates Wisdom and signifies that the maiden acts not blindly but with full knowledge of her power.

The lion symbolizes the most powerful force in nature, the procreative urge, which rules all living things below man, and which man must subdue and control with his mental force, and thus rise to the angelic plane mentioned in the Bible, where they neither marry nor are given in marriage (Mat. 22:30).

The purpose of the whole ensemble is to symbolize that power over the degenerative and destructive aspect of Creation which Man acquires by knowledge, but which few men have the will-power ever to use. The major portion of this power should be directed to the subjugation of the procreative urge of the body, on which power we have much to say in our work titled the Great Red Dragon, and concerning which Levi wrote:

"To control the allurement of generation (procreation) is to graduate in the conquest of the body, and supreme chastity was the most glorious crown set before the Hierophants" (History of Magic. P. 134).

The most notable reference in the Bible to the principle portrayed in Tarot Card No. 11 is the remarkable fable of Samson. His amazing Strength lay in his chastity. He slew with his hands the angry lion pictured in that card, and later took honey from its carcass;honey being symbolically the substance the Celestial Body receives from the purity represented by the highest work of the bee.

In plainer terms, Samson subdued the procreative urge of the body; and the bees, or the Creative Process, utilized the Life Essence conserved by his Chastity to increase his Spiritual Strength by the consumption of that Essence in the brain to increase knowledge, instead of consuming it to increase the population of the earth. The great philosophers produce philosophy, not families.

Samson's mental struggle with the body's procreative urge
struggling in the brain is cleverly represented in the Bible as
"war in heaven." Michael and his angels, symbolizing the Celestial
Phase of the Mind in the brain, fought against the Dragon, symbolizing the body's procreative urge, and resulted in victory for the
Higher Mind; and so, all influences of Carnality were subdued, and
"neither were their places found any more in heaven" (Celestial
Mind) (Rev. 12:7,8).

As long as Samson remained pure in Chastity, he was boundless
in Strength. But when ye yielded to carnality, his Strength waned.
In this fable the Bible says:

"And the lords of the Philistines came up unto her (Delilah),
and said unto her, Entice him, and see wherein his great Strength
lieth, and by what means we may prevail against him,that we may bind
him and afflict him, and we will give thee every one of us ELEVEN
hundred pieces of silver" (Judges 16:5).

The evidence shows that the compilers of the Bible knew what
they were doing and had the secret of ELEVEN. They used ELEVEN
chapters in Genesis to cover the long space of time from the Creation down to Abraham, the great Chaldean Astrologer; and they used
him to begin a New Cycle that gave birth to a New Tribe, which divided
into Twelve Parts as symbols of the Twelve Signs of the Zodiakos.

Concerning this Mott wrote: "The Twelve Fathers of the Hebrew
Nation were (only) astrological characters (and not real people).
A reading of the 49th chapter of Genesis could leave no doubt on that
score" (Meaning of the Zodiac, p. 98).

The Bible ends with Revelation, which was divided into 22 chapters, double 11, to correspond with the 22 letters of the Hebraic alphabet; and in the 11th chapter thereof the Temple of God was opened
in heaven, and there was seen in his temple the ark of his testament;
and there were lightnings, and voices, and thunderings, and an earth-
quake, and great hail.

Now think of modern science, groping in darkness, and calling
these Wise Masters Superstitious Heathens because the essence of their
parables goes over the head of our great scientists.

In his book, The Sacred Tarot, C.C. Zain wrote: "The three times
Samson was bound and easily broke his bondage signifies that the

powers of purity prevail in the physical, and the astral and the
spiritual realms. Hair is coincident with the (body's) age when
sexual (creative) virility is attained (manifested), and Samson,
having been unshaven from birth, indicates his natural ability, due
to purity (chastity) of Life, to use his virile (creative) force in
a constructive manner. But Delilah was a harlot, and robbed him of
his purity (creative essence), (and thus symbolically) shaved him
of his constructive (creative) powers, and delivered him into the
hands of his enemies (carnality), and they put out his eyes" (spiritual sight) (Judges 16:21).

The name Delilah is Hebraic and means "the weakening or debili-
tating one." The word comes from the Hebraic Lilah, which means
"darkness," "night," and with D or De prefixed, the name Delilah is
formed. The Hebraic D, "daleth," is the fourth letter of the Hebraic
alphabet and means Door. And so, Delilah is "the door to darkness,"
which, in ancient mythologym means dense matter.

Delilah made Samson "sleep upon her knees; and she called for
a man, and she caused him to shave off the Seven Locks of his
(Samson's head; and she began to afflict him, and his Strength went
from him" (Judges 16:19).

Consider the blind stupidity required on the part of any intelligent person to accept such biblical fables as literal facts. Samson was a mighty heavy sleeper; for he knew not that he was being
shaved. Preposterous.

Ancient fables, invented by the Superstitious Heathens, to teach
definite facts of Life and Creation unknown to our vaunted scientists, and accepted by a brainwashed people as factual history. It's
not surprising that we fall into one ditch after another in accepting
literally the ancient mythology and symbology presented in the
Bible. Here is what Coulson Turnbull said about it:

"Biblical statements have three meanings that can be communicated orally or by symbol. A fourth exists, gained by a method of
inner sight known to the trained mystic. The four meanings are concealed in the word Paradise, which word represents the three planes
of involution of the archetypal world. It also represents Eden,
a word denoting pleasure and delight, everywhere the pleasure received
from the overshadowing power of the Elohim, grafting and planting
the germ prepared that the Soul of Man should be made upright.

"Eden and Paradise really mean a prepared (celestial) garden
for the Soul, in which it should enjoy Divine Activities. Paradise
is made up from the letters P-R-D-S.

"1. PASHUT, the material or exoteric religion composed of blind illusions of the material world and the senses. The first five books of the Bible are written in this sense, hence their difficulty of interpretation.

"2. REMMEZ, an advanced step, using allegory and partly veiled statements.

"3. DERSEH, a higher step in understanding with a fuller interpretation of the hieroglyphs, allegories and symbols.

"4. SOD, the fourth letter in Paradise was not communicated orally but gained only by Souls in the loftiest state of contemplation.

The reader should consider how misleading it is for one to read the Bible and believe literally what one reads in it.

Chapter No. 12

Aquarian Age

In Chapter 7 we mentioned the Zodiakos, describing its dual wheels and their relative differences.

The Earth is now leaving behind the last degree of Pisces, the Water Sign, and entering the first degree of the Air Sign, called Aquarius.

Under the influence of the Water Sign upon the Earth and its inhabitants, the inventions of man in the last 2000 years have related to water--the canoe, the water wheel, dams on streams to generate power, steam engine, steam ship, etc.

With the advent of the Piscean Age, which began about 255 B.C., there soon appeared the birth of a new religious system. But its clever founders declared that it was not new--just the ancient Pagan System revamped and renamed. The facts supported the declaration, for its Hero exhibited the same symbolical nature, the Sun of God, but, under the influence of the Water Sign, a Fish was the first symbol of him, and he was surrounded by Fishermen.

Rev. Dr. Geikie, in his "Life and Words of Christ," said that a Fish stood for his name, from the significance of the Greek letters in the word that expressed the idea, and for this reason was called a Fish. A clever explanation to conceal basic facts.

This Hero of the Piscean Age spent much of his time on the water and around the sea of Galilee. He was represented as being a native of Galilee, an area located a considerable distance north of Jerusalem. According to the gospels, his chief food consisted of fish and bread, and this same type of food he fed to the multitude represented as following him.

As the polar opposite of Pisces is the Material World, the Piscean Age has been a crude materialistic one, in which a doctrine of Spiritualism has been preached from the pulpit, but its true nature not understood, in which right was wrong, truth was error, and blind faith annulled all mistakes.

Fortunately for humanity, that Age is nearly over. The Earth is entering the Aquarian Cycle, and the next two thousand years will be a period of advancement, enlightenment, intelligence, an era of faith in stable facts with known substance, instead of empty creeds based upon superstitions.

Witness the many signs already appearing to indicate the changing order, as the Earth passes from the influence of Pisces, the Fish and Water Age, to that of Aquarius, the Fruit and Air Age. The change that has already come is amazing, and is sweeping forward so fast that it has now become practically world-wide.

All leading nations are taking to the Air, the consumption of Fruit has increased amazingly in just the last generation, and the old Pagan Religious System, which was given a new name as stated, is now mustering every ounce of its fading strength in its struggle to survive the sweeping changes which are threatening its existence.

The struggle will fail, for its days are numbered and its doom is definite as the world order changes under the influence of the Celestial Bodies which rule the Earth, its inhabitants, and the ebb and flow of its oceans.

One astonishing achievement of the New Aquarian Age is the splitting of the Atom. In that event science suddenly discovered that Matter is not what it was thought to be. Matter turned out to be an illusion, for it may be convered into its fourth state, pure heat, and pass into the imponderable, thus revealing the fact that what we know as Matter is just concentrated, congealed, solidified gaseous substance, under the influence of Polarity, and by the application of heat, may be dissipated, vaporized and caused to disappear completely from sight.

When Matter, as vaporized substance, disappears from sight as incandescent gas, that is all that was, that is, and that will be of the Creative Elements. For when it congeals and thus becomes visible, it forms the four phases of substance which the Masters, for convenience, termed fire, air, water and earth, and symbolized it by the Sphinx, the image of which is found in all nations of the ancient world.

But we must constantly keep in mind one salient point about which we shall have more to say in due time. Regardless of how vaperous and invisible Matter may become, its final stage of apparently Incandescent Gas is the Fiery God that keeps the "flame of life" burning in the cell of every living thing, and that Flame is the Vital Force of the animal.

The splitting of the Atom revealed the secret of inner knowledge of all things which the world sorely needed, in order to explode

the preposterous concept of physical science as to the actual nature
of Life.

We now have conclusive evidence that Life is more than a "mode
of motion," more than the "expression of a series of chemical changes
in the body." And until we recognize this later knowledge and apply
it to all living things, we will remain superficialists, groping
about in a world of darkness as the Christian World has been doing
for sixteen hundred years.

And if the ancient inscription on the Pyramid of Gizeh says,
"I am all that was, that is, and that will be; no mortal man has
raised my veil," it may now be replied thereto that modern science,
in splitting the Atom, did unknowingly raise that veil, and was
shocked to find that Force and Matter were, now are, and will always
be the Dual Aspects of the Universe.

It has been this knowledge of the actual nature of Matter that
has long been needed to solve the secret of Creation. And it marks
the turning point in the long descending process of the Dark Ages.
From here on the movement will be upward. But that movement will
be slow and painful, for the few Travellers on that Path of Light
must battle valiantly and constantly against the retarding, obstruc-
ting, materialistic dogma of a smug and stubborn science, entrenched
in all the schools and colleges.

The recent annihilation of Matter, as such, has annihilated
that ridiculous, grotesque, physico-chemical concept of Life, postulated by physical science and espoused by medical art. The gateway
is now open for an intelligent, scientific, metaphysical philosophy
in which both Spirituality and Materiality may be recognized and
assume their respective places.

Life is the Knower, yet, strangely enough, the physical scientist has wilfully ignored the existence and presence of the mighty
Factor by which he is conscious of his own existence. "I cannot
explain why I am alive rather than dead," said the great Dr. Millikan.

Manly P. Hall said: "Through the study of man, we can discover
the conscious Living Universe. And by the contemplation of univer-
sals, we can come to appraise the complete human being who, like the
great figure of the Zohar , stand with his feet upon the earth and
his head among the stars.....

"Man can never attain security until he understands his relationship to the causal world above him and within him. Wisdom alone

bestows sufficiency, but Wisdom is meaningless until it leads to the solution of the mystery of Life" (Planetary Influence).

The Four Elements of Creation, symbolized by the Sphinx, are called the Sacred Four in the most ancient scriptures. Col. Churchward said he found references to the Sacred Four in the Sacred Inspired Writings of Mu, the lost continent (p. 65).

The King of the Sacred Four appears as Fire, said to be the Absolute Reality, the inner nature of which was discovered in the splitting of the Atom, and found to be power so violent, that the Hebrews called it El Shaddai (terrible power), and the Hindus called it Jaggernath (ruthless power), as we have said.

The Sacred Four Elements receive due notice in the Hebraic Kabbala, and are indicated by the four letters, J H V H, called the Sacred Word, the Ineffable Name, which we have discussed in chapter 8.

The evidence indicates that the God Almighty (JHVH) of the Bible, the El Shaddai of the Hebrews (Ex. 6:3), and the Jaggernath of the Hindus, is the Universal Power of Creation that is devoid of all moralized consciousness to perform any action but Creative Action, according to preordained plan, regardless of consequences or cost,--all of which knowledge was possessed by the Masters and duly recorded in their scrolls and scriptures. Hence, to mention God as Love is the climax of civilized stupidity and theological nonsense.

Take a look at the fossilized remains of prehistoric animals and men of past geological ages; yea, of destroyed cities and even entire civilizations, which abundantly testify of the determined and ruthless processes of Creation. Nothing can bar the forward march of Creative Action.--and the end is not yet. More civilizations will be wiped out before the existence of the earth ends in that final explosion previously mentioned.

If the destruction of living things is necessary for the progress of Creation, or their degeneration is essential to preserve and perpetuate the species, so be it.

This aspect of the subject was briefly mentioned in Chapter 10, where it was stated that if it were not for the protective atmosphere of the Earth, the Creator's Consuming Fire of the Glorious Sun would destroy us a hundred million miles away.

The fable relating to Samson indicates to those who can interpret it, that carnality is one of the worst enemies of physical man, as the Ancient Masters knew it to be, and worked faithfully to warn him of its serious consequences. They said in their immortal allegory that in the day thou sonsumeth the Creative Essence of the body, dying thou shalt die (Gen. 2:17).

The great Pythagorean philosopher Paul was aware of the dangers of carnality, and in some of his Epistles he disclosed that he knew the secret meaning of the Edenic Parable. In his Epistle to the Romans he declared:

"The commandment which was ordained to life (procreation), I found to be unto death" (Rom. 7:10).

Paul referred to the commandment in the very first chapter of Genesis, "be fruitful and multiply"(vs. 28). And he showed by what he said that he knew Propagation produces Degeneration and Premature Death:—

"O wretched man that I am," cried Paul, "who shall deliver me from the body of this death" (Rom. 7:24).

There is no escape; but there is a deferment that may be gained by the practice of Chastity and Self Denial. And by this means of refusing to procreate, the days of the flesh may be greatly prolonged. Man then rises to the high Angelic Plane where "they neither marry, nor are given in marriage, but are (liberated from the body's creative urge) as (are) the angels of God in heaven" (Mat. 22:30).

The Great Sacrifice

How little the masses do know about the requirements of the Law of Life, and how little do they understand the precious Pearls of Ancient Wisdom, scattered throughout the Bible,which teach us that masturbation and fornication are serious Sacrifices of the Essence of Life without recompense. There processes consume and squander the most vital substance manufactured by the body, whereas if conserved, it would greatly benefit both body and brain, making sages of such men, and gods of the race.

The various fables referring to this subject begin in Genesis, as the mythical Tree of the Knowledge of Good and Evil (Gen. 2:17), and in the last book of the Bible the fable mentions the Pale Horse whose Rider is Death (Rev. 6:8).

The interpretation thereof: The Pale Horse symbolized the lowest mental department of the body, and Death, the Rider, signifies the procreative function. "For in the day that thou eatest thereof (dying) thou salt surely die." And so power was given unto them" over the fourth part of the earth, to kill with sword, and with hunger, and with death, and with the beasts of the earth."

Since that ancient fable was first written, the masses have steadily declined into sexual debauchery, and it is conservative to estimate that now this power rules half of civilization, instead of one fourth, if not more.

We discover the hidden meaning of the biblical ideograms by studying Creation and Creative Processes. The flowers of the field decay in the function of production, and die as they seed. But science fails to realize that this is Sacrifice in obedience to the commandment, "Be fruitful and multiply."

Under this phase of the Creative Cycle, Man begins to degenerate and decline when he begins to serve that commandment. His slow, downward course to the grave commences when he begins to consume in masturbation and fornication his precious Creative Essence.

In 1934 we wrote a correspondence course of 85 lessons on that subject, and that was our first failure in the field of health literature. Talk and write about anything you please, but shun everything that relates to carnal lust.

Production of offspring is the Great Sacrifice mentioned frequently in the Bible, but not understood by the clerics and laics. Man weakens his body and brain and shortens his days as he consumes his precious Creative Essence in pleasure and procreation. One noted author asserts that this alone cuts two hundred years from the human life-span.

Goddard E. Diamond died in 1916 in San Francisco at the age of 120, and was unable to explain in his book on his long life, which he wrote in 1904 when he was 108, why he lived so long. He thought his use of Olive Oil was the cause of it and gave oil the credit. The big secret in his case lay in the fact that he never married and did not consume his Life Essence in pleasure and procreation.

The Ancient Masters understood the secret of the Great Sacrifice. But nothing as to its true nature is taught in the schools or churches. It was constantly under attack by the Masters, and Paul hit it some hard blows in his Epistles to the Romans, especially in the 5th, 7th, and 12th chapters. And no doubt what he actually said was softened and modified in the Bible. He shouted:

"I am carnal (in the flesh), sold under sin (be fruitful and multiply)....bringing me into captivity of the law of sin (procreation) which is in my (generative) members.....(yet under the law you must) present your bodies a living sacrifice, holy, acceptable unto God, which is your reasonable service" (to obey the command "be fruitful and multiply") (Rom. 7:14,23; 12:1).

Concerning the Great Sacrifice, Dr. F. H. Curtiss wrote: "In ancient times when a place of worship was to be established, a more or less conscious recognition of the Law of Sacrifice was observed, for the first stone to be laid was the Stone of Sacrifice.

Curtiss then added: "This law (of Sacrifice) is also illustrated (rigidly observed) in the ceremonies of Initiation into the (Ancient) Mysteries, during which the Neophyte must (most solemnly swear to) sacrifice (the function of) the lower, personal man; and must allow it (the creative urge of the body) to(die and) be dead and buried" (by taking a most solemn oath completely to subdue forever the procreative urge of the body and yield not) (Message of Aquaria, p. 257).

This brings us to the basic reason why the Ancient Mysteries, after functioning for thousands of years, were finally destroyed by the Roman Emperors in the 4th, 5th, and 6th centuries A.D. For they would not be accepted for Initiation unless they met and submitted to the fixed requirement NOT TC "BE FRUITFUL AND MULTIPLY." That they positively refused to do.

And so it came to pass that the Ancient Mysteries were finally outlawed and abolished, and such of the Masters who did not flee and hide, were killed. The bitter feeling against them was intensified by falsehoods to the point where those were persecuted and assassinated who showed any sympathy for the Masters or any consideration for their teachings.

And this harsh rule was applied to the Initiates who did not forsake and repudiate the doctrine of the Ancient Mysteries. It was these Proselyted Initiates who were the original workers in the establishment of Christianity, and also the original compilers of the Bible. Paul was one of the great leaders of the group, and he had been one of the leaders of the Ancient Mysteries, being Initiated in Greece, Egypt and India. And included were Demas, his beloved disciple, and Luke (Lucian) and Mark (Marcion) (Col. 4:14; Philem. 1:24).

Begotten of God

In his book, Evolution & Regeneration, Henry Proctor, F.R.S.L., M.R.A.S., of London, wrote:

-105-

"Whosoever is begotten of God (Virgin Birth) does not practice sin, because his seed remaineth in him, and he cannot sin, because he is begotten of God" (1 John 3:9).

After paraphrasing that from the Bible, Proctor then added:

"We know that the seed, retained in the body (and not consumed in procreation) is transmuted into vitalizing fluid, the (only) Elixir of Life (on earth), which increases (the power of) life in the body, in every part, first in the physical, then in the mental, and finally in the spiritual."

Wise men search not for the Elixir of Life without the Kingdom of God, for the Kingdom is within, and it includes all for man and his body's requirements. Be not misled and deceived by the doctors and their dope.

The Kingdom of God is located within the form of flesh called the Temple of the Spirit of God (1 Cor. 3:16), and the wonderful Elixir of Life is made by the body itself, and consists of the precious Creative Essence consumed and expended in procreation and in pleasure.

Wise men do not thus consume their Elixir of life and then expect to recover their loss by attempting to replace it with some substance that is of little value to the body, and more often harmful.

Tarot Card No. 6, titled Temptation, was devoted to this subject.

In one of the most noted Temples of the Ancient Masters, all that is symbolized in this card was expressed in symbolic ceremony celebrated every evening at sunset. It was performed by a pure virgin Priestess who had been educated in the Temple and protected from all profanation. This highly important matter has received due attention in another work and will be bypassed here.

So lacking is scientific teaching on the Great Sacrifice, and so frail is puny man to cope with the inexorable laws of Creation, and so little does he know of these laws, and so little do his teachers and leaders know of these laws, that he is more helpless in the grip of these laws of Creation than are the lowly bugs and birds, which know enough about the requirements of these laws to live in harmony with them, consequently they are never sick, have no hospitals, no doctors, no drugs, no vaccines, no serums, etc.

What do our supposedly great schools and colleges teach that is of much value to Man in matters of health and life? When but a few of the facts of Creation are presented and considered, it is readily realized why degeneration is so rampant, why people are sick so much, and why they die so young; and why such a small minority of the best of the race ever rise to higher levels of Consciousness and become sages and seers. And for the sake of their own safety, they must hide in silence. For what they know and practice is so foreign to what is taught in the schools, that they would be misunderstood, would be branded as enemies of civilization, and cast into prison.

The same multitude which took up stones to stone Jesus is still here with us (John 10:31). The methods may change with time, but not the motives.

The honor and respect accorded the Mental Giants of all ages by their fellowman, is never compensatory for the great effort involved and the Self Denial exercised in the subjugation of the greed, sensations, jealousy, lust and evil of the flesh, in order to gain the higher goal.

This particular phase of Creation is so vital, that it is covered in another very special work that interprets the fable of the Great Red Dragon of the Bible that stood before the woman, who was ready to be delivered, "for to devour her child as soon as it was born" (Rev. 12:4).

The Red Dragon symbolizes the most powerful force in Nature, which holds totally in its grip the vegetal and animal kingdoms, and which the Masters discovered how to conquer, to control, and to divert its power from Destruction to Construction.

The secret of their greatness was their discovery of ways and means to shift the lever, making the Creative Force work for them instead of against them.

Wisdom

With the splitting of the Atom there came increased need for Wisdom. "For my people are destroyed for lack of Knowledge," says the Bible (Hosea 4:5).

And Wisdom, says the Bible, is better than gold or weapons of war (Pr. 16:16; Eccl. 9:18). Yea, Wisdom is far better than precious stones; and all the things that may be desired by man, are not to be compared to Wisdom (Pr, 8:11).

For the mysterious and imponderable nature of the Creator has been found to be such that, lacking Wisdom, he who discovers the Creator will be destroyed by Him.

Science exhibits more of its stupidity when it holds that the biblical concept of the Creator belongs to the primeval days of the race, when man lived in caves and killed beasts with stone-hammers.

That opinion existed before the discovery of radio-activity, of cosmic radiation, of astral light, of electrons, of the terrific power of the tiny but mighty Atom.

Today, as the scientists of the New Aquarian Age examine the so-called foibles of antiquity and the "heathenish concept" of the Creator, they are amazed to discover that the inspired Seers of by-gone ages were truly illumined with conceptions of the basic facts of Creative Manifestation which the latest researches are beginning to prove were correct, although these conceptions were often expressed in dramatical, poetical, symbolical, and allegorical terms.

Infinite Force, now termed Cosmic Electricity for want of a better name, is the primeval substance of the Universe, and the only visible manifestation known of Absolute Reality--the Unknowable Reality of the Evolutionists and physical scientists. And the Created Phenomena called Nature, which is the visible effect of the transmutation of Infinite Force, are the manifestations to Man's consciousness of the Creator.

It should be remembered that the Bible says that no man can see the actual Creator and live (Ex. 33:20, etc.). This statement is now better understood due to the Wisdom gained by the experiance of the splitting of the mighty Atom.

The ancient hypothesis of the Creator is symbolized in Card No. 4 of the Tarot, titled the Emperor, and mentioned in Chapter 8. The Interlaced Triangles symbolized the unition of the Creator with His Creation, which signified the ancient concept that Created Phenomena are visible manifestations of the creative work of the Creator. Strictly speaking, it is more of a Visible Reflection of the Invisible Pattern.

One shrewd author said: "Causation is infinite and eternal. Transformation (Creation) is the product of what the world calls Creation. The Creative Cycle, called the Wheel of Life by the Masters and symbolized in Tarot Card No. 10, is in constant motion like the constant motion of the Earth and the Sun. Its work never begins and never ends, and extends from the Invisible World to the Visible World and back again in an endless stream."

ASTRAL LIGHT

Chapter No. 13

KING FIRE

"I sense One Flame, O Gurudeva. I see countless undetached sparks shining in it" (Secret Doctrine, Blavatsky).

King Fire, master of all forces, greatest of all elements, reducing all substance to incandescent gas, was logically the leading symbol in the Ancient Wisdom of the Fiery Creator of the Universe.

After the proud Temples were demolished and the priceless Scrolls were destroyed then by the Army of the newly established Mother Church to obliterate the Ageless Wisdom, the precious fragments thereof lay buried for centuries beneath the rubble of the cities in which the Flaming Torch of King Fire had been so gloriously hailed as a Symbol of the Fiery Creator.

Evidences of this symbol still appear in the humblest hut in the East where there is always a Light that never fails, physically or symbolically, the terrestrial reminder of the Eternal Creator.

For similar reasons a Light constantly burns before the Holy Ark in the synagogue; and there is a Light over the Altar of the Church, and one illuminating the Crescent of the Mosque. In more ancient times there was always a Light upon the hearth.

The Giant task of compiling the Bible from the scrolls of the Ancient Astrologers was begun by that great man Eusebius of Caesarea (264-349 AD), a renowned scholar, a learned leader, some say an Initiate of the Ancient Mysteries, and Emperor Constantine's right-hand bower at the First Council of Nicea in 325 A.D., where and when there occurred that epochal event of the founding of the Roman State Church, not so much as a religious institution as a political expediency , according to the real facts of hidden history.

Time has proved that this great trick by Constantine was unwise. It failed to do what he wanted it to do. And when the shocking news reached Rome of what the Council of Bishops had done at the distant city of Nicea, it made the leading Romans so angry that their surly reaction constrained Constantine to remove his headquarters from Rome, and "built a new capital on the site of an old city of Byzantium," wrote Monsama, "and it was named for the founder, Constantinople. He made this a Christian city, building churches in every quarter and eliminating all reminders of (ancient)paganism" (p. 86).

This awful error of Constantine laid the foundation of the bitter religious wars that swept his vast kingdom, finally causing the Fall of Rome, and ultimately plunging Europe, Egypt and Asia Minor into a sad state of darkness that lasted for a thousand gloomy years.

Had Eusebius lived to finish the Bible, it had been a far differend book than it turned out to be. But he died before it was completed, and the work was taken over by Jerome (331-420 AD) and finished in the early part of the Fifth Century.

Jerome lacked much of being the polished scholar that Eusebius was. He was not so proficient in knowledge of the meaning of the ancient symbols and allegories as Eusebius was. This caused him to include and exclude certain scriptures, the value of which was questionable to him, and to give the wrong slant to many of his interpretations of the ancient language.

But regardless of who had made the Bible, none of the biblical scribes in those turbulent times had dared to commit to writing in lucid terms the secret knowledge concealed in the ancient symbols and allegories.

And so, the Bible was not compiled by the Founders of Christianity to present, in overt detail, the Ageless Wisdom of the Masters, but to conceal it. Hence, there is much truth in a remarkable book of 800 pages by Krypton, titled Quartum Organum , wherein he declared,

"The Bible is nothing but (ancient) mythology, and when we come to deal with it (which he did in the later pages of his book), we will prove that it is plagiarized mythology at that" (p. 320).

The Christian World erroneously believes that this mythology is of Jewish origin. But no reference to any Jews occurs in the Bible until we reach 2 Kings 16:6. Why the theologians call Abraham, Isaac and Jacob "Jews" is difficult to understand. For no Jews were known in history during their days. This is just another instance which proves how badly mistaken the theologians are on many things that appear in the Bible.

Another amazing feature of the Bible is the adroit manner in which fictional and factual propositions are interwoven and inter-blended to such an extent, that we defy anyone to read one chapter or one paragraph in the book, and point out the faction and the fiction separately stated.

Every fiction in the Bible is inseparably linked with an undeniable fact, and the twain are so intricately blended that it is utterly impossible for the unprepared mind to separate the one from the other.

Making the Bible was a huge undertaking and a delicate task. The compilers did not relish the proposition of recording those profound secrets of the Ageless Wisdom that had always been passed on orally from generation to generation and never committed to writing. No sane member of the Masonic Lodge would dare to put on paper the secrets of his Order that are always whispered from ear to ear.

That is the principle reason why it took years to make the first draft of the book. The compilers were confronted with the task of recording for the first time, those features of the Ageless Wisdom that had never before been put in writing. It had to be done in such an ingenious manner that the exoteric could not detect the hidden meaning of what they read, and yet think they did. And so, every word, every phrase, line, sentence and paragraph had to be studied with extreme care, to make the messages misleading to the exoteric while informing the esoteric, and still conceal from the eyes of the world the hidden meaning of the symbols and allegories.

Revelation, last book of the Bible, is one of the most stupendous allegories ever penned by the hand of man. It has steadfastly baffled the best brains of the Christian World to decipher its hidden meaning. Even Krypton, extra wise in biblical lore, failed to find its secret message when he took it apart in his book mentioned above.

And the work of revision and interpolation of the Bible has never ceased. Since about 1880 when the Revised Edition of the King James Bible of 1611 was published, there have been numerous other versions published by groups that have special theories of God and His work, such as Jehovah's Witnesses, who want the Bible to show the world that their postulates are the "real McCoy."

Then the press of September 21, 1952, carried this statement: "Religious events of 1952 include the publication of the Revised Standard Version Bible." And thus the scheme goes on, with various reasons offered as excuses why it is done.

But why should such unbounded importance be attributed to the Bible or to the tyranny of words? The Bible is only a book that has been made by man; and no book, no author, no pastor, no group, no organization can vary or change the facts of Creation. For those fixed facts we are here searching. They are far more important, valuable and trustworthy in man's life than any book, regardless of its age, source, author or nature.

Books cannot alter Creative Action, change human life, nor confer immortality upon man. Even the Bible cannot do that. For that is the realm and work of Creation alone, and is governed strictly by cosmic law. No book is valuable except as it presents the facts, the laws, the processes and the secrets of Creation.

We are the Children of Creation and not of the Bible. Our Father is not the Pastor of some church, but the Creator of the Universe. Our origin, nature, and destination are not determined by the Bible, nor ruled by any Creed formulated by a Council of Bishops. All of that is determined by Creation and ruled by Cosmic Law.

The basic processes of Creation produce everything known and unknown, and they never change. They are changeless, eternal, in constant operation, and operate the same today as they did a million years ago. They will operate the same a million years hence as they do now. Certainly, we need no bewhiskered prophets to juggle that simple fact.

And then what is the most vital of all points for which the world is searching? Why do millions of people attend church? For a dependable answer to that great question posed in the Bible, whether a man who dies shall live again (Job 14:14).

Give humanity a definite answer to that burning question and the Bible may be burned. And where can this great answer be found except in the facts, laws and processes of Creation?

Ancient Wisdom, sacred scriptures, religious systems, creeds, doctrines, dogmas, belief in crucified saviors and faith in resurrected gods may be good business for the clergy, but they do not rule Creative Action nor govern human life. They change not the immutable, inexorable, inflexible, fixed and changeless laws of Creation. And that is well for humanity.

The Great Mystic

In the entire Bible it appears that Paul presented the best answer of all to the great question posed in the Job, and postulated it in its simplest form in his first Epistle to the Corinthians.

This makes it proper that we know something about Paul's background in order to determine his state of competency in such a weighty proposition as the one before us.

Who was Paul? He is first called Saul in the Bible; and then, without a word of warning, he suddenly becomes Paul (Acts 7:58; 13:9). There must have been a reason for that.

Valuable data dug from the ancient rubble reveal a surprising story of this man. His real name comes up as Apollonius, a fact the Church has tried hard to hide. He was a Pythagorean Philosopher,the greatest mystic of the First Century, lived to be almost one hundred years old, and did nothing but study, write and preach all his life.

He spent much of his time in Antioch and Ephesus, and it is said that he was at Ephesus when his demise occurred. And in order to obliterate all traces of this man and his work, history states that none of the ancient cities have ever been more completely destroyed than Ephesus.

The New Testament was chiefly compiled from his voluminous writings, which were salvaged by Marcion, the Mark of the Second Gospel, who was an educated and influential Cappadocian, whose native language was the Samaritan, and he said he found the writings of Apollonius in Antioch after the latter's death.

Apollonius was the leader of the Essenes, and they suddenly disappeared from history after Christianity was born. Their, history goes back thru the Pythagorean Greeks and on to the ancient Hermitic Brotherhood of Egypt, founded ages before by that legendary personage called Hermes Trismegistus. This organization was primarily known as the Order of Melchizedek, the Children of the Sun or the Sons of Light (Gen. 14:18; Ps. 110:4).

The story of Apollonius (Pol, Paul) appears in the works of Philostratus, translated from the Greek in 1870 by C. L. Kayser at Leipzic; also in Antiquity Unveiled, published in 1894; and in The Gospel of Apollonius by K.S. Guthrie, M.D., published in 1900.

With dependable data showing that Paul actually lived as stated, and that he was a Pythagorean Philosopher, we have the Key to the background of his valuable writings and teachings. But they are twisted and distorted in many instances in the Bible, with deliberate breaks here and there in the context that are filled with spuriour interpolations to incorporate statements never made by Paul.

To our surprise, it is admitted in the Bible that Paul was a minister of a very ancient gospel, which, he declared, has been preached (for thousands of years) to every creature under heaven (Colossians 1:23).

Of course, a gospel of such antiquity was not the more modern gospel contained in the New Testament, which is so recent as not to be more than three centuries old. And so Eusebius, the first Christian historian, was constrained to admit that Christianity was not new, but just the old pagan system under a new name.

The Pythagoreans observed the ancient philosophy of the Astrologers, that Fire constitutes the Heart of the Universe, the Monad or First Form, and extends from the earth to the uttermost reaches of the Cosmos. They held that all created phenomena are the product of Fire, and strive ever to return to Fire.

This goes directly back to King Fire of the Atlantean Masters, to whose doctrine Paul strictly adhered. He wrote that God is a Consuming Fire in his Epistle to the Hebrews, following the same statement that appears in Deuteronomy, written perhaps two thousand years before his time (Deut. 4:24; Heb. 12:23).

The very first religion of which we have any accurate account is that of Atlantis. It was the Fire Philosophy, and the Solar Orb of the Universe was regarded as the Father of all, making us Children of the Sun. And so, in the Bible the Psalmist sings a lyric unto the Sun, as follows:

"The Lord (of Fire) reigneth; let the earth rejoice; let the multitude of isles be glad. Clouds and darkness (in the sky) are round about Him (Sun).......A Fire goeth before (floweth out of) Him. His lightnings enlighten the world; and the earth saw, and trembled. The hills melted like wax at the presence of the Lord (of Fire)..... The heavens declare His righteousness, and all the people saw His glory." (Ps. 37:1-6).

H. P. Blavatsky wrote: "The esoteric teaching sayeth that Fire is the perfect and unadultered reflection in Heaven as on Earth of the Divine Flame. It is Life and Death, the origin and the end of every material thing. It is Divine Substance.....

"The secret of Fire lieth hid in the second letter of the Sacred Word (J H V H). When the power point (of the Interlaced Triangles) vibrates, when it glows, when the point, the center, and the apex connect and circulate the Fire, when the three fold apex likewise Flames, then the Two Triangles (the Blazing and the Black), the greater and the lesser, merge into one Flame, which consumeth the whole (Secret Doc.).

Dr. R. S. Clymer said, "All the early Fathers (of Christianity) considered the Creator to appear as Subtle Fire....Without Fire and the resultant heat, there would be no existence. Fire and the Soul are One and the same thing--the Living Fire" (Philosophy of Fire).

The Living Fire was the Philosophy and Religion of the ancient world. That was the pagan gospel which had been preached for thousands of years to every creature under heaven, whereof Pol was made a minister, "after the order of Melchizedek" the Priest--King of (Jeru) Salem (Ps. 110:4).

That pagan gospel now lies buried beneath the rubble of the temples of antiquity. But fragments of it are preserved in the Bible and in other ancient lore, and can be identified by the few who understand the mystery of Creation and the secret of Life.

The ancient Fire Philosophers, which included the biblical Pol, held that everything transcends into Fire. All things are derived from Fire by rarefaction and condensation, the one active and the other passive, the one synthetic and the other analytic.

Heraclitus (535-475 B.C.) taught that as all things are derived from Fire, they are eventually transformed again to Fire.

The Ancient Astrologers said, "From Fire to Earth and back again, an infinite number of worlds are born, only to suffer annihilation (by explosion) in due course, succeeded by reconstruction and re-destruction without end." This of course implies that the entire Universe is "Fire in the process of endless transformation."

The renowned Kabalist Eliphas Levi wrote:

"All (ancient) Assyrian symbols (are connected with the Science of Fire, which was the great secret of the Magi. On every side we meet with the enchanter who slays the lion and controls the serpents. The lion is (a symbol of) Celestial Fire, while the serpents are (symbols of) the electric (positive) and magnetic (negative) currents

of the earth. To this same great secret of the Magi are referable all
the marvels of Hermetic Magic, the extant traditions of which still
bear witness that the mystery of the Great Work consists in the ruling of Fire" (His.of Mag. p. 56).

Dr. A. E. Waite quoted from a very ancient work on Fire as follows: "When thou dost behold the Sacred Fire with dancing radiance,
flashing formless thru the depths of the world, then harken to the
Voice of Fire" (p. 67).

Fire was the most ancient symbol of the Creator and of Life,and
the greatest of all purifying agencies known. In the Egyptian
Mysteries there was a symbolical purification of the Neophyte by the
Sacred Fire.

The initials I N R I of the Latin sentence which appears on the
Cross, and is translated Jesus Nazarenus Rex Judaeorum, were used by
the Rosicrucians at the initials of one of their Hermetic secrets,
"Inge Natura Renovatur Integra". (By Fire, Nature is perfectly re-
novated.)

These four letters are also the initials of the Hebraic names
of the Sacred Four Creative Elements, Iaminim (water), Nour (fire),
Reuch (Air), and Iebschah (earth).

The Flashing Flame darting upward into space to meet its Celestial Counterpart, is the Terrestrial Fire seeking ascension to and
absorption in the Divine Fire, and constituted the Flame Secret of
the Fire Worshippers. This is the universal religion that passed
from the sunken continent of Lemuria to India, thence to Egypt, Asia
Minor, Palestine, and Greece, the traces of which appear in the
Bible.

The Lord of Fire appeared unto Moses in a Flame. The voice of
the Lord spoke to Moses from a bush that burned with Fire, and was
not consumed. The Lord descended upon Mr. Sinai in the midst of
Fire; and Fire was a symbol of the Creator in the ancient scriptures.

The fundamental doctrine of the ancient religion of the ancient
world was the veneration of the Sacred Flame, and above all, Astral
Light, the purer, brighter atmosphere of the Astral World, the Vital
Breath of the Universe which animates the Living World.

The Living Fire of the Universe was held by the Ancient Masters
to exercise its Creative Action thru the Sun as its focal point, during the Sun's revolution along the signs of the Zodiakos, with which
signs unite the paranatallons that modify their influence and concur

-116-

in finishing the symbolic attributes of the Great Luminary of the
Universe, which rules and regulates all Creation and all Created
Phenomena, called Nature, and is the depositary of all Creative
Forces.

The Encyclopedia Americana (1938) said, "The terrific energy
of Fire, the most important (and most active) agent known, the
similarity of its effects with that of the Sun, its intimate connection with Light, its terrible and yet genial power, and the beauty
of its changeful flame, easily account for the marked reverance in
which it was held in ancient times."

For what else should any civilization, ancient or modern, show
more reverance than that which should be known as the most important
and most active agent in the Universe? If more time and money were
expended in the study of King Fire and its processes, we might then
develop a science that would be more useful and constructive than
the present system of speculation erroneously called Science.

If we can discover and determine the destiny of things, that
knowledge solves the secret of their origin. The fore-ordained future of all objects of bodies is revealed by definite knowledge of
their primal origination. For that data completes the Creative Cycle.

The observation and experience of thousands of years show that
ignification changes every substance, from water to stone, to a state
of incandescent gas that vanishes from sight and forms the atmosphere
in which the earth floats. And there goes that solid, material
world of science, and there, in a few simple words that can be comprehended by a child, is revealed the origin and destiny of all
things known.

All physical substance is condensed incandescent gas, and the
degree of condensation extends in regular order from the most dense
substance known, as stone and steel, to the rarest, called Fiery
Ether.

Electrified gaseous substance is said to be the primal element
of which are constituted suns, stars, planets, moons, subjects and
organisms, including the mineral, vegetal, animal and humanal kingdoms. It is the one universal element that binds together the diverse
particles called Matter. It is the inextricable network of vibrations, waves, and influences, of numberless, nameless, and uninter-
rupted fluids that connect everything known with everything that
exists.

Electricity is the cosmic element which has never been clearly
defined nor properly recognized for what it is. Science shows that

-117-

it exists primarily in two distinct states--concentrated in the form of electrons and protons, and waves classified as radiation.

Heraclitus said the element called Life is "a portion of Universal Fire (electricity) imprisoned in a body constituted of earth and water," and Hippocrates declared that "Life is a Flame burning in water." He regarded Heat as the foundation of all Life.

The Hebrews, copying from their more advanced neighbors, said that all things are the progeny of Fire, and regarded the Creator as Consuming Fire.

F. J. Mott wrote: "This Macrocosm-Microcosm doctrine is quite alluringly simple. According to it, the Solar System is the Macrocosm, whilst Man is the Microcosm. The one reflects the other and is seen in the other. Therefore, so the hypothesis runs, if we can read the one we can also read the other" (Meaning of the Zodiakos, p. 9).

Fire is eternal and the King of all the elements. The historians exhibit their ignorance when they write about man's discovery of Fire. For Fire has been belching forth for billions of years from the numerous volcanos of the earth, and Vulcan was the ancient god of the Fiery Element.

Fire is the greatest and most dangerous force known. Yet man himself could accomplish little without it. With Fire he has cleared the jungled wilderness and transformed the forest into productive fields. All his most useful tools of metal are fabricated by the use of Fire. With Fire he drives his steam-ships, locomotives, motor cars, trucks, busses, bulldozers and airplanes.

And by the aid of Fire man has strayed from his native home in the tropics and lives a brief and artificial existence in the hostile land of ice and snow, where he spends his precious days in grinding toil to keep from his door the ever present Economic Wolf--created by his own stupid transgression of the law. And this leaves him little time to devote to the development of his Mind and the acquisition of Knowledge.

Daily toilers for subsistence are self-made economic slaves. Their enslavement increases in direct ratio with the decrease in land production. That fact explains why those in the cold zone must toil all the time to battle with the economic problem. Where frost and freeze are unknown, and droughts do not destroy, there Creation produces abundantly, and little human labor is needed.

In our southern states the natives work less than people in colder regions, and in the tropics the natives do relatively little labor because of the great economic freedom they enjoy. But their leisure leads to laziness, and laziness leads to degeneration; hence, good health and long life is a rare exception among such people.

Fire and Light were the leading elements of the Masters. The Pantomorphic Fire was considered by them as the Creative Power of the Creator, and was called Astral Light. Hence, it is logical and consistent that all ancient religious regarded Fire as the direct manifestation of the Creator, deeming the Sun the Universal Fire.

Fire to produce heat in some degree is absolutely essential to every manifestation of Life. Without Fire, all would be cold and lifeless. At absolute zero (273^0 C.), scientists state that all manifestation ends, the atom then being entirely at rest.

As Fire is an aspect of Divine Radiance, Life is a manifestation of the Creator. Wherever there is Life, there the Creator is in manifestation. The Bible says, Whither shall I go from thy Spirit? Or whither shall I flee from thy Presence? If I ascend up into heaven, Thou art there; if I make my bed in hell, behold, Thou art there. If I take the wings of the morning, and dwell in the uttermost part of the sea, even there shall Thy hand lead me, and Thy right hand shall hold me" (Ps. 139:8,9).

The Bible also says: "Ye came near and stood under the mountain; and the mountain burned with Fire unto the midst of heaven, with clouds and thick darkness. And the Lord Spake unto you out of the midst of the Fire; ye heard the voice of the words, but saw no similitude; only ye heard a voice....For the Lord thy God is a Consuming Fire" (Deut. 4:11,12,24).

Clymer wrote: "Fire appears as the chosen element of God. In the form of the flaming bush He appeared unto Moses. His presence was denoted in torrents of flame; and in the form of Fire He preceded the Israelites by night thru the dreary wilderness." Just another allegory.

"By Fire we can alter solids; part them, powder them, melt them, drive them out to more and more delicate and impalpable texture--firing the invisible molecules, or imponderables, into clouds, into mist, into gas; out of seeing, into smelling; out of smelling into nothing" (Jennings).

The Bible says, "There went up from the earth (under the influence of heat), a mist and watered the whole face of the ground. And the

Lord God formed man of the dust of the ground, and breathed into his nostrils the Breath of Life, and man became a living soul." (Gen.6:7)

"This mist," wrote Dr. F.H. Curtiss, "was caused by heat (Fire), making the water to evaporate and moderating the cold. Hence, only as Fire entered as a third constituent of the earth, could (the body of) man be made of 'dust of the ground.'

"Since to manifest in each world (terrestrial and celestial), the Soul must necessarily have a vehicle or body composed of the substance of that world. To manifest on the earth, a physical body must be perfected, composed of the same material as the earth is, or literally 'of the dust of the ground,' ere the Soul can function on the terrestrial plane. Since man then contained (in himself) all the elements of manifestation, he became a Microcosm or Cosmos in minature. 'As above, so below.' And thus it is that heat (Fire) completes man. No creation can be completed until the force of heat (Fire) has done its perfecting work" (Key of Destiny, p. 297).

As the first age of the Earth was the Solar Age, so the primary religion of which we have any accurate account was the Fire Philosophy of the Atlanteans, as we have said. It was an absolutely philosophical religion, when Science and Religion walked hand-in-hand as brothers, as dual expositers of the Cosmic Unit, and men knew that they manifested within their own body the Divine Fire of the Universe, the Power which characterizes those great ones who raised themselves up by celibacy to the Angelic Plane, high above the Animalistic Kingdom (Mat. 22:30).

The Bible reveals that back in that early day, the Despots were there and were engaged in the regular course of persecuting and murdering those who worshipped the true Creator instead of some popular Idol. The Bible says, "O son of man, turn thee yet again, and thou shalt see greater abominations than these. And he brought me into the inner court of the Lord's house, and, behold, at the door of the temple of the Lord, between the porch and altar, were five and twenty men (Masters), with their backs toward the temple of the Lord, and their faces toward the east (as the Masons face unto this day), and they worshipped the Sun (of God) toward the east" (Ezekiel 8:15,16).

And what happened when the Despot's spy made this report? The account shows that the old charge of Idolatry was hurled against the Masters, and the usual decree went out from the ruling Despot to "slay utterly old and young, both maids and little children."

In 1881 an unusual discovery was made that revealed an interesting phase of ancient religion. Researchers, in their work of excavating in the ruins of an ancient city in Asia Minor, discovered, among other treasures, a clay chest containing an artistically inscribed alabaster tablet, in six columns, decorated at the top with a skilfully executed bas-relief.

In this Holy of Holies, a god with flowing beard, symbolizing the Creator, held in his right hand a ring (symbol of Eternity), and in his left hand a staff (the Caduceus, symbol of the Creative Principle), was seated upon a Throne, the arms of which were decorated with the head of a Ram, as pictured in Card No. 4 of the Tarot, titled The Emperor, which we have discussed in Chapter No. 8, titled Tetragrammation.

A king, followed by two priests, approaches the God in adoration, while two other men are raising a Sun Disk with ropes upon the roof of the Temple.

It was a valuable discovery, as it revealed the character of certain phases of the Ancient Wisdom, and perhaps more so because this document also disclosed the name of the building and also a very ancient city. An explanatory legend on the bas-relief said:

"Image of the Sun God, symbol of the great Lord, who dwells in the Temple of Ebbars in the City of Sippar."

Amazing; one of the most ancient Babylonian cities had been discovered, in which Noah-Xisusthros, by command of the God Kronos, was ordered to bury the documents of antediluvian days.

The Temple of the Sun of Ebbars which, from the time of the foundation of the city of Sippar until long after the days of the last of the Chaldean kings, was the center of Solar Worship in Babylonia ; and the great interest of concern of all the ancient Babylonian kings had been recovered.

This discovery takes us way back and reveals a vista into the ancient past of mankind on Babylonian soil which reaches beyond the time of Abraham, the Chaldean Astrologer who was born in that land, and whose fabulous story begins with the 12th chapter of Genesis.

In all of the ancient scriptures from which the Bible was compiled, Fire regularly and consistently appears as a symbol of the Creator. The lights on the altar are symbols of the Creator; and as Fire and Light are identical, so Fire was always the symbol of the Grand Architect.

Chapter No. 14

REFLECTION

The Book of Ecclesiastes of the Bible indicates to the esoteric
that it was the work of a Master. It presents peculiar passages not
found elsewhere in the Bible.

The word Ecclesiastes means speaker, debater, preacher, and the
book discloses to him who can think, the revealing observations of
ancient science. It declares that things which appear mysterious are
only natural results of natural causes; that like causes produce
like effects; that the Created reflects the Creator; that birth and
death are but words that refer to the surface aspect of Creative
Action, and are ruled by an immutable power that rolls on forever.

There is a strange reference to a Silver Cord and a Golden Bowl
(Eccl. 12:6). The clerics may think this cord was a necklace for
the queen, and the bowl was a goblet in which servants prepared special beverages for the king. That little do theologians know about
the biblical symbolism. For they are taught that the Bible deals
chiefly with God and Heaven, and for these they look in that book.
But the Masters who wrote the ancient Scrolls were interested in Man
and Creation, two great subjects of the world in which priests and
pastors have little interest.

What is Man? How can the clergy know when science admits that
it does not know. The great scientists freely admit that to them

Man is a mystery. They say man is constituted of a procession of
phantoms, in the midst of which there strides an Unknowable Reality.

Those frank statements of ignorance mean the Christian World has
no Science of Anthropology and Biology. So we are forced back to
the Bible for reliable data as to the nature of Life and the constitution of Man. Even then we can learn little unless we are competent to interpret the strange symbols and allegories of the Bible,
for they conceal from the exoteric the very things that we want most
to know.

We are lost in the fog of ignorance unless we can sensibly interpret such symbolism as the bush that burned with fire and was not
consumed; of four living creatures that came up out of the sea; of
Jehovah; of Jacob's Ladder; of the Golden candlestick with bowl on
its top; of the Book with Seven Seals; of a door opened in heaven;
of seven angels, seven vials, seven last plagues, and seven thunders;
of a New Jerusalem coming down from heaven; and there shall be no
more death, nor sorrow, nor crying, neither shall there be any more
pain; for the former things have passed away.

All this symbolism deals directly with Creative Action, with
Life and its processes, with Man and his body, with Birth and Death.
But the Christian World never heard a sermon in which any of this
symbolism was presented and interpreted according to the doctrine of
the Ancient Masters.

Symbols were invented and used by the Masters to conceal from
all but the Initiates, certain vital knowledge relating to Creation.
The Bible is a book of such symbolism, with many spurious interpolations of the biblical compilers to mislead the exoteric. And no author
in modern times has ever interpreted that symbolism to our knowledge,
because no modern author has possessed the ability to enable him to
do so.

The best that has come to our attention in this field is the
various works on the interpretation of the symbolism of the Ancient
Tarot. And not one of them, in our opinion, has interpreted that
symbolism strictly in harmony with the designs and doctrines of the
Masters who invented it.

And furthermore, no Master and no Initiate ever dared to comit
to writing, any interpretation of that symbolism. Its esoteric nature
was preserved by the most powerful sanctions. An oath of secrecy was
taken, in the most serious form, in the Ceremony of Initiation. To
violate that oath was considered a sacrilegious crime, the prescribed
punishment for which was immediate death. And the record shows instances of the execution of that death penalty.

Count Eugene Goblet d'Alviella wrote a book titled Migration of Symbols; and when he died in 1925 at the age of 79, he was recognized as "the greatest exponent of symbols." His work is valuable in many respects, but it makes no attempt to analyze the ancient symbolism. No doubt his knowledge of the mysteries of Creation and the nature of Life was insufficient to enable him to do that. When science can't tell what Life is, it is assumed that he did not know. And without that knowledge, one is not competent to interpret the ancient symbolism. For that is the chief subject with which it deals.

According to the Bible, after the Noachian Flood, God set "My bow in the clouds, and it shall be for a token as a covenant between me and the earth,....and I will look upon it, that I may remember the everlasting covenant between God and every living creature of all flesh that is upon the earth" (Gen. 9:13-17).

Here is an important symbol, related directly to Creation. An analyzation thereof reveals valuable data relative to Creative Action and the Creator. As that data affects the entire Universe and everything in it, it will disclose the very things we want to know about the secret of Creation.

Whence cometh the Rainbow with its seven colors? Is it an independent Entity, or a dependent Effect? Does it spring from substance and return to substance? or does it spring from nothing and fade into nothingness?

In this simple example of Creative Action, the entire mystery of Creation is revealed. Due to the darkness in which Men walk regarding such things, this simplicity is so great as to be unbelievable . Yet the same simplicity applies to all Creation, from the Rainbow, the Created Object we can see. And we realize that all qualities manifested by the Rainbow are those of Astral Light, the Creator.

The Rainbow is an Effect created by Astral Light, which is invisible, eternal, omnipresent, and neither comes nor goes. If there were no Astral Light, the Creator we cannot see, there would be no Rainbow, the Created Object we can see. And we realize that all qualities manifested by the Rainbow are those of Astral Light, the Creator.

The Created can present not real nor essential attributes which the Creator does not possess. The Effect can draw its reality and existence only from the Cause, which must contain in itself at least all that is essential in the Effect. Dependent and derivate, the Effect bears, in itself the evidence and the condition of its dependence.

In the absence of the Rainbow, we would not know that Astral Light, the Creator, existed and possessed these various attributes. And so, by this illustration we learn the Creator can be known only by His work. Never in any case can He be known otherwise. Hence, we should stop searching for Him, as the great scientists and religionists have done.

By analogy, the case of the Rainbow and of Astral Light discloses the secret of the Creator, of the Creation, of the Created, of Man, and of Life. We thus know that Man is a created object. He is not an independent Entity, but a dependent Effect. He is a formation created by the Creator who is invisible, eternal, omnipresent, and neither comes nor goes.

THE CREATOR IS CONSTANTLY PRESENT IN HIS CREATIONS.

Were there no Creator which we cannot see, there could be no created Man which we can see. And all the mysterious attributes seen in Man, come from and are those of the Creator, precisely as in the case of the Rainbow.

If it were not for Man and for all created things known, we could have no knowledge of the Creator, nor of all those attributes which are such a puzzle to the great scientists, and which are said to spring from nothingness and return to nothingness.

Thus we learn the value of symbols, and the wonderful story they unfold to him who can interpret them. It would require a big book to relate in detail the marvelous story of the Creator that is revealed by the Rainbow to him who understands.

Kingdom of God

When the author, or perhaps the interpreter, of the Ancient Scriptures wrote, "The Kingdom of God is within you" (Luke 17:21), he would have operated on a level but one step higher in his understanding had he omitted the one word "within." And human history for sixteen hundred years would be far different from what it has been.

If the schools taught what Man should know about Creation and himself, he would realize that his body is not him, and that he has no body in the death phase of Creative Action.

By an anlysis of this point, we may be much surprised to learn that the Creator in the body is the power that Looks, and it cannot see that which does the looking. That which Looks can see only some

created object other than itself. It can never see itself, for IT
HAS NEVER BEEN CREATED.

All that which is seen by that which Looks has been created or
it would not be present to be seen. Like the Rainbow, everything
that can be seen by that which Looks, has been created and is visible,
and anything which cannot be seen by that which Looks, has not been
created and is not visible.

To an intelligent, unprejudiced person who can think, that may
seem simple. But, as we said, it is the fundamental simplicities
which are always difficult to accept, because they are so very simple,
and therefore, unbelievable on that account.

It is obvious from logical reasoning that there is only one fundamental prerequisite to seeing anything in the physical Universe--
it must be created like the Rainbow for instance.

This second simplicity can readily be accepted. And by further
analysis, it grows definitely certain that things not seen have never
been created. By experience we know that what has never been created
can Look, but that which Looks has never been created.

In summarizing: That which Looks is uncreated and eternal, and
that which is seen is created and temporal, as the Bible says (2 Cor.
3:18). As all objects that can be seen are created and have dimensions, that which Looks is uncreated and has no dimensions.

There are but two definite states of existence, and both are
mentioned in the Bible: The Seen and the Unseen, the Temporal and
the Eternal. That fact the Bible presents in these words:

"We look not at the things which are seen, but at the things
which are not seen; for the things which are seen are temporal, but
the things which are not seen are eternal."

The Creating Force, unseen, uncreated and eternal, can co-exist
only with a counter-force, which is the created object that can be
seen. And the existence of either without the presence of the other
is an utter impossibility. This means that they cannot be separated.

This brings us directly back to the primary proposition: "The
Kingdom of God is within you." The premise, the reasoning, and the
conclusion are consistent and clearly indicate that THE KINGDOM OF
GOD IS YOU THAT LOOKS. That assertion is confirmed by the Bible in
these words:

"Know ye not that ye (body) are the Temple of God, and that the
Spirit of God dwelleth in you (your body)? If any man defile the

Temple of God (body) him (body) shall God destroy; for the Temple of God is holy (being the home on the earth of the indwelling Spirit), which Temple ye are" (1 Cor. 3:16).

"What? know ye not that your body is the Temple of the Holy Ghost (Spirit) which is in you (and which is you), which ye have of God, and ye are not your own? For ye are bought with a price; therefore glorify God in your body, and in your spirit, which are God's" (1 Cor. 6:19).

That price is the imprisonment of the Creator in corruptible flesh so that He may appear on earth in the flesh in the midst of His Creations.

It is the body that is defiled and not the Spirit, and it is not the Spirit but the body that snall be destroyed. The destructive action begins at birth, and the body slowly sinks in a steady process of deterioration that ends in premature death of the body. So badly does the world need a school to teach man how to care for the Holy Temple to make it a fit place for the indwelling of the Creator in the visible world. We learn how to care for the Holy Temple of God by learning the requirements of the body and supplying them, and not in the study of the body's derangements.

By no effort or study or thought, ever so long continued, can we become conscious of any entity within our body that is separate from us, from our brain. For only He that Looks is the one who lives in the body.

This doctrine agrees with what H. P. Blavatsky said when she wrote:

"Throughout the whole range of mystic literature of the ancient world, we detect the same idea of Spiritual Esotericism, that the personal God exists only within the worshipper, and never without. That personal Deity is no vain breath, nor a fiction, but the immortal Entity."--Sec. Doc.

This assertion does not mean that no manifestation of the Creator appears outside of the body. It means that no personalized Creator appears outside of the body.

The Immortal Entity in the human body, as a Ray of the Creator, is analogous to a Ray of Sunlight as an individualized manifestation of the Sun. Just as the Ray becomes individualized in flower and fruit, so the Animative Ray of the Creator becomes individualized in human flesh, inhabiting the form of flesh as the Ego, the Spiritual

God, the Lord from Heaven, as the Bible says, and doing the work on the earth plane which man erroneously thinks that he does.

Just another one of the many illusions of Creation; and the visible world is full of them. Misunderstood because we are not properly taught, and because we see not what we think we see.

We are taught from childhood to believe that we exist as separate objects, standing apart from the Creator. Even the great scientists are as badly fooled as the lowest layman. They think they are the Looker when that Looker is actually the Creator for whom they are looking, and declare that He is a myth because they cannot locate Him.

Biblical statements appear to mean nothing at all to the Christian World when the evidence shows those statements declare the facts of Creation.

The Bible definitely states that the human body is the Temple of the Holy Spirit; but the Christians refuse to believe it. That Spirit creates the body, as an instrument for its use, that harmonizes with the environment, and thru which to act and function on the earth plane, as the Bible says.

And so, when the bald facts are faced and understood, we comprehend the deeper meaning of the scriptures, that God created Man in His own image and likeness. In plainer terms, God walks and works on the earth plane in the form of flesh called Man, and that explains why Man is such a mystery to the scientists and to himself, and why science has never been able to classify him, calling him an animal, but admitting that he is not.

Hence, only as we present and recognize the facts of Creation, and identify ourselves as the Focal Center of the Divine Incarnate Ray of the Creator, can we comprehend that we are just the illusionary Effect of the Holy Spirit that inhabits the body, as the Bible says. Only when we are able to open the Book of Life, sealed with Seven (Incarnate) Seals (Rev. 5:1), and read it with understanding, and realize the meaning of its mystic message, converse intelligently with the bee and the bird, and understand the Music of the Spheres.

The Masters employed many tricks to hide from the exoteric their remarkable knowledge of Man and the Creator, such as the passage that God created Man in His own image and Likeness. We find the hidden meaning of that message when we realize that God appears on the earth in the midst of His Creations in human form.

Where would we reasonably expect to find God if not in His work? How could He appear with the fruits of His labor without an instrument that harmonizes with the environment? And what sort of a body could be better adapted to His purpose than the human body?

The gospel Jesus understood these things when he said, "He that hath seen me (Man) hath seen the Father,.....(for) I and the Father are one" (John 10:30; 14:9).

Jesus represented Man, and Man and the Father are ONE. This explains the reason why science has never been able to classify Man, calling him an animal as we said, but admitting that he is not. His body presents animalistic characteristics, but his Mentality is definitely not that of any animal, such as thinking, planning, reasoning, inventing, etc.

The philosophers of all ages have declared that while Man stands with his feet upon the earth, his head is in the stars--meaning that although his body exhibits animalistic properties, his Mind presents the exalted qualities of the Creator.

Where shall we search for the Creator? In His Holy Temple, the Human Body. He who refuses to accept this Doctrine should destroy his Bible, for its Blazing Beacons are meaningless to him.

Man, the climax of all Creation, comes into existence in the mother's womb, as if by magic, from an invisible particle of Electrified Substance, commonly called the Solar Spark, which is the Animative Ray of the Creator.

As all the qualities of Astral Light, the Creator, are manifested in the Rainbow, likewise the qualities of Astral Light, the Creator are manifested in Man, in the highest degree. For that purpose Man is made and for that use he is here. This explains what we are and why we are. "Lo, I come to do thy will, O God" (Heb. 10:9).

The superior qualities of the Creator which appear in Man are a mystery to science. These qualities are called Vitality, Consciousness, Mind and Intelligence. In no medical book on earth are these qualities logically described or sensibly defined In fact, we are told they do not exist--except in the imagination.

Thus does science solve the problems of Life. We are assured by science that we live in a Universe deprived of Life and Consciousness, and constituted of blind and unknown forces. Where will we go if we follow that kind of science? Where are we now as a result of following that kind of science?

We know without question that the qualities of the Rainbow are those of Astral Light, its Creator. We must be very ignorant if we cannot understand that the qualities of Man must be those of the Creator.

We know the Rainbow has no existence apart from Astral Light, its Creator. We should understand by analogy that Man can have no existence apart from the Creator. Shall we believe the Bible when it says that in the Creator we live, and move, and have our being?

As the Rainbow is but a reflection of the qualities of Astral Light, its Creator, so Man is but the reflection of the qualities of the Creator. And that which may be known of the Creator is "clearly seen" (in Man) said Pol, "being understood by the things that are made" (visible) (Rom. 1:20).

If our schools were not dominated by a materialistic science that scorns Spiritualism as the fallacy of Superstitious Heathens, we would know better than to search for the Creator. What we need is to be taught how to recognize Him.

That is what Pol tried to do in what he said. But we now live in a different world, where Ancient Wisdom is regarded as Heathenish Superstition, where stupidity has replaced sagacity, where Matter has replaced Mind, where fallacy has replaced factuality, where materialism has replaced spiritualism.

Listen to the words of the great scientist, Dr. Alexis Carrel: "The Mind, hidden within the living matter, is completely neglected by physiologists and economists, almost unnoticed by physicians, and yet it is the most colossal power in this world. (And yet) Matter has been separated from Mind (by physical science and) to Matter has been attributed a greater reality than to Mind" (Man, The Unknown).

Thus we observe that science has reversed the actual situation. Mind is the Reality and Matter is the Phantom. Mind is the unseen and the eternal, and Matter is the seen and the temporal.

When we consider the fallacies of modern scientists with the factualities of the ancient scientists, we readily understand the reason why we live in a world of darkness and ignorance, of confusion and speculation, where the scientists are searching here and there for the Creator, and claiming that He is a figment of the imagination because they could not find and can not find Him.

"The ancient doctrine of Omnipresence," said Emerson, "meant that the Creator appears in every bee and bird, in every moss and cobweb."

In His created objects the Creator is logically limited to the functions thereof. In the human form He is restricted to the organs

-130-

of the body and is served by them. He can communicate with created objects of the earth only by the intermediation of the body and its organs. The body is an instrument, adjusted to the physical environment in which it is created, and in which the Creator works and walks upon the earth.

By thus confining and restricting the action of the Creator, it makes possible His activity in the physical world. In the absence of the body, He would be everywhere, like air released from a truck tire, and yet in so rare a state that He could not act definitely anywhere. He must have an instrument thru which to function.

Imagine a drop of fresh water sealed in a globule and cast into the sea. As long as the container remains intact, the drop of fresh water will subsist in its separate form. But let the globule be broken, and where shall we look for that drop of fresh water in the vast ocean?

The Creator must create bodies for His use, and He can endow them with self-conscious personalities only by restriction in an instrument, so as to centralize action and, by restriction, concentrate the operation.

When the body becomes unfit for His use, the Creator leaves it in the Born Again process called Death. And He changes environment of necessity, ascending Jacob's Ladder clad only in an Astral Garment, or vehicle of Astral Light, and ascending by reason of His nature, just as air rises from water in escaping from a broken bottle immersed in water.

We say the Creator ascends because the vehicle, in which He is clad, ascends and because function and consciousness are both inherent therein. The function and consciousness of the Creator can manifest only by means of that instrument thru which the Creator acts. These qualities of Life manifested by the Creator do not belong to the instrument. It is the instrument that is used by them.

The atmospheric air is condensed for luciferous bodies which are infinitely rarer than it is, and they could descend only by assuming a grosser vehicle, which they could not obtain in the region above the earth's atmosphere. They could return to earth only by means of another incarnation, and such return would be a lapse, for they would be renouncing their state of unlimited freedom and renewing their novitiate.

The ancient doctrine here presented was formulated by the Masters in a single axiom: The Creator clothes Himself to come down to the earth, and disrobes Himself to ascend Jacob's Ladder. And this is the actual interpretation of that symbolism.

The Death of the body frees the Creator from the magnetic attraction of the earth, called Gravity, by which, while inhabiting the body, He has been bound to the earth.

The ascent of Jacob's Ladder begins in the darkness of the earthly atmosphere, and mounts toward the Sun, the Cosmic Creative Agent, which was symbolized by the Masters by the Sun, and the journey to the Sun being nothing more or less than symbolical.

And the eternity of the Creator cannot be a state of inertia. For the Creator passes from virtue to virtue, from bliss to bliss, from victory to victory, from glory to glory, from finitude to infinitude.

The Most Startling Revelation of the Age!

Chapter No. 15

Astral Light, in the form of lightning, pierces dark clouds and the resulting peals of crashing thunder shake the earth.

Astral Light, intensified as heat, vaporizes the diamond and transforms all objects to incandescent gas that disappears from sight.

This mighty power of Creation is symbolized in various ways in the Bible, but that symbolism presents little interest to the exoteric, yet it conceals the great secrets of the Universe.

We get a better impression of the situation by realizing that the Ancient Masters were top level scientists, who knew we live in a Universe of law and order, and who outclassed by far the best scientists of this age.

The Masters held that the Powers of Creation are reflected in the things created. That is the fundamental doctrine of Omnipresence. It means the Creator appears in every force, every form, every element, every object, every plant, and every drop of water.

The Masters had gods, but their gods were not personalities. They were symbolical in character and were invented to represent the forces and elements of Creation. The carvings on their Temples and Stone Monuments, not subject to any change and far older than the oldest scriptures of the Bible, show that their principle God was the glorious Sun, the gigantic generator of the Universe, without which there would be nothing, and with which there is everything.

-133-

This knowledge is preserved in the Bible, which says, "For the Lord thy God is a Consuming Fire. For the Lord most high is terrible, He is a great King over all the earth" (Deut. 4:24; Ps. 47:2; Heb. 12:29, etc.).

This moralless Creator is not a God of Love, but is so fierce and terrible that if it were not for the protective atmosphere of the earth, we would be destroyed a hundred million miles away. There would be no means of escape, and the Bible tells us that in these words:

"Whither shall I go from thy spirit? Or whither shall I flee from thy presence? If I ascend up to heaven, thou art there; If I make my bed in hell, behold, thou art there. If I take the wings of the morning and dwell in the uttermost parts of the sea, even there shall thy hand lead me, and thy right hand shall hold me" (Ps. 139: 7-10).

We should consider these meaningful statements deeply and not pass over them lightly, for in so doing we miss the very points for which we are searching.

By symbol and allegory the Masters connected the Sun with all Created Phenomena, which we call Nature and do not understand what we mean by the term. This symbolism appears all thru the Bible, but is meaningless to the clergy.

The clergy never connect with Creative Action such symbolism as a Door Opened in Heaven, the Silver Cord, or Jacob's Ladder. To the Clergy, the basic meaning of this symbolism is a profound mystery.

1. The Door Opened in Heaven (Rev. 4:1) may be the port of entry into the World of Eternal Bliss and Endless days; and--

2. The Silver Cord (Eccl. 12:6) may be a cable for man to scale in his ascent to his Heavenly Home, and--

3. Jacob's Ladder (Gen. 28:12) may be an alternative way of getting up to Heaven.

For the orthodox are taught that Heaven is a place and how to get there is the chief concern. Hence, they wink at the statement in the Bible that Heaven is a condition of the mind and not a place in space (Rom. 14:17).

The Bible says, "My people are destroyed for lack of Knowledge" (Hos. 4:6), and that is the true situation today.

It is erroneous and misleading to believe this biblical symbolism has no other meaning than that of reaching a Heavenly Home in the
sky. It conceals some great secrets of Creation, but the clergy are
incompetent to determine that fact when they know practically nothing
about Creative Action, and nothing basic and sensible concerning it
is taught in the schools or by science.

We have got to be unorthodox to discover and understand the
secrets of Creation; and we are going to be so unorthodox as to assert and to show that the symbolism mentioned--

1. Deals directly with Creative Action, and
2. Leads directly to the mysterious Creator,
3. So deeply hidden from the orthodox, and yet
4. Appears on the earth in Human Form exactly as stated in
   the Bible, to the effect that:-
5. Got created man in his own image and likeness.

If such statements in the Bible mean anything, what do they
actually mean? That we shall explain so clearly that even a child
can understand.

Ancient Wisdom

According to extant fragments of the Ancient Wisdom, Anaximenes
(526 B. C.) said, "The Essence of the Universe is in Astral Light in
eternal motion, which contains ALL IN ITSELF. Everything is formed
by integration and disintegration of the Essence of Astral Light under
the Law of Expansion (heat) and Contraction (cold)."

It required the discovery of wireless telegraphy and radiophany
for science to recover this lost knowledge and bring back to us some
data of the Astral World of the Masters, which contains the essence
and germ of everything that appears upon the earth as Created Phenomena.

The biblical makers excluded from the Bible much which the ancient
scrolls contained regarding the Astral World in order to keep man in
darkness as to his fundamental nature, incorporating some minor passages which tell the unprepared mind nothing of the secret of Man
and Creation.

It seems to mean little to the clerics and less to the laics to
read about Pre-Existence in the Bible, to the effect that every plant
of the field (was in the astral world) before it was in the earth,and
every herb of the field (was in the astral world) before it grew (in
the earth) (Gen. 2:5).

Immutable law and consistency of thought demand that there be included in this category of Pre-Existence not only the vegetal kingdom, but animals and human beings,--pre-existing in the Astral World as Archetypal Entities prior to their appearance on the earth in physical forms.

For the Law is One, the Source is One, the Substance is One, and from this One proceeds all of the known and the unknown.

Something comes not from nothing. What is called Creation is a process of transformation, in which the potential becomes the actual, the invisible becomes the visible, as invisible vapor becomes visible water.

Man does not come from nothing. He is a materialization of an Archetypal Entity of the Astral World, and every part of his body is formed by the Condensation of Astral Light, and not of what he eats and drinks. The tree that appears to come from the apple seed is not the product of what the seed eats and drinks, but of condensed Astral light.

The Nerve System

It is essential for the purpose of telling Man what he is to consider in details the mysterious Nerve System of his body, whose "wires" exceed in extent all the commercial wiring in the world, and are charged with a force that is a great mystery to science.

We are now at the point where the ignorance of science is glaringly displayed as to the nature of Life and the constitution of Man. As we wade thru this data the reader will receive many shocks.

What are the Nerves? Science says they are sinews or tendons, and they begin in the brain and end in various parts and organs of the body. Little is known of their nature, their function, or their importance, and not much attention is given them by the doctors, except the chiropractors.

For one thing, we are going to learn the reason why no system of caring for the sick has ever grown so fast as chiropractic has. Accidentally discovered in 1895 by Dr. Daniel D. Palmer, its amazing growth is due to the fact that it deals with the Living System of the body; and the chiropractors will be amazed when we show them that, in treating the sick, they are actually dealing with Astral Light, flowing thru the Nerves as electrical currents.

When the chiropractic schools were founded a little more than half a century ago, they had to use medical text-books because there were no others. And these were found, by the experience of the chiropractors, to be so faulty as to the Nerve System, that they were discarded and replaced by books prepared by leading chiropractors, the chief of whom was old Dr. Willard Carver. And then that wonderful work published in 1933 by Dr. E. J. Livingstone.

It is very obvious that if the Nerves began in the brain as science claims, the Vitality, Consciousness, Mind and Intelligence of the human body would be one of the greatest of all miracles. And that is exactly what these qualities are to science, to theology, to the whole world. Thousands of writers have sought to explain the nature of these qualities and their origin.

Peruse all the medical text-books in the world, as we have done for sixty years in our search for the secret of these qualities, and in them there is nothing concerning these qualities of Man that satisfied an intelligent person.

While almost nothing definite is known by science about the nature and source of these qualities, yet they are the qualities that make Man what he is; and if we know nothing about these source and nature of these qualities, we can know little about Man, his origin, his nature, and his destiny.

And so, quite logically we find great scientists frankly admitting that they cannot define Life, that Unknowable Reality as they term it. Dr. R. A. Millikan said, "I cannot explain why I am alive rather than dead."

Is Life such a mystery? or is there something hidden under the cover? For instance, what would happen to theology and medicology if the secret of Life were known? There is a reason for this ignorance.

When we follow science in the quest of Life, we march into a world of darkness. That is where the scientists are and admit it. And where are the clergy who preach from the pulpit their dogma of Eternal Life? They are in the same boat with the scientists.

If the Nerves did begin in the brain, as science claims, whence cometh the qualities of Life we have mentioned? Medical art cannot answer that question. Medical institutions have failed to solve the most elementary lesson of Life. This means that no doctor, unless he be a chiropractor, is competent to treat the sick.

According to science, the Nerves begin in the brain, and Nerve Force, Vitality, Consciousness, Mind and Intelligence originate in some unknown way in the brain. The brain is a great organ, but it's not that great. Nothing can present what it does not possess.

Science asserts that these qualities seem to rise from body function, and vanish into nothingness when body function ceases. Now, if that is science, what is "ignorance." Perhaps Ignorance becomes science when expressed by a scientist.

Back in 1616, when Wm. Harvey, physician to the king of England, shocked medical art with the announcement of his discovery of the circulation of the blood in the body, he could not complete his discovery by determining how the blood passes from the arteries to the veins, as no connecting tubes could be seen by the aid of the best microscope available.

Harvey knew the blood must pass from the arteries to the veins, but he could not explain the process. For the arteries seemed to end in nothing, and the veins seemed to begin in nothing--just as the Nerves seem to begin from nothing in the brain. There seemed to be no connecting tubes between the arteries and the veins.

Learning little from that experience, medical art goes on teaching that the Nerves begin in the brain, converge at the medulla oblongata portion of the brain, and there form the spinal cord, which extends down the canal in the spine, with Nerves branching from it all the way down, and going out thru the body and to all the organs and glands.

The Ancient Masters were too astute to be deceived by the illusion of sight. They used their mind and they knew in their mind that the Nerves could not begin in the brain; for they are charged with a force that does not and cannot originate in the brain, and is not and cannot be generated in the body, as science claims.

Now for another secret of Creation: The Brain and Nerves are sinews and tendons that are composed of congealed Astral Light, the same Light which creates the Rainbow. Yea, that Light which produces the Rainbow with its Seven Colors not only creates the Brain and Nerves, but the entire body of the infant in the mother's womb.

It was the discoveries of Littlefield, Crile and Lakhovsky in the realm of Astral Radiation that gave the modern world, for the first time, a sensible Law of Animation.

These men showed that what we call Life is a state of activity , a "mode of motion" as Herbert Spencer called it, resulting from

Astral Light flowing as electrical current thru the Nerves. And science stubbornly refuses to recognize that fact.

Man, the copyist, makes metal wires to convey electricity, thus following the pattern of Creation. His own body has "wires" which receive and convey astro-electricity to all organs and parts of his body, and makes him a Living Soul.

Electricity is an aspect of Astral Light. It is the most mysterious, most powerful, and most dangerous force known. It presents good and evil phases, the results produced depending upon the conditions supplied.

The atom is held together by tremendous electric voltage. When the atom is cracked, these voltages are released in the form of energy. In the atom bomb dropped on Japan in 1945, the atoms of uranium or a similar substance were broken in two--liberating the astrounding energy of 200,000,000 electronic volts per atom.

The action of Electricity is limited only by the mechanism thru which it functions. It heats water and freezes it, turns wheels and luminates globes, runs clocks and rings bells, drives trucks and airplanes, animates animal bodies and executes them.

A vast electro-magnetic field surrounds the earth, called its Aura. It is created by Astral Light contacting the earth's magnetic emanations, and is so dense that it has a pressure of almost 14.7 pounds a square inch at sea-level, unnoticed by man because his body is made to resist it.

This was the Astral World of the Masters. From it come all living things on the earth, and to it these things return in the Creative Cycle, called the Wheel of Life by the Masters, and symbolized in Card No. 10 of their Tarot.

In the creation of Man, the brain forms first in the mother's womb by the condensation of Astral Light. As the condensing process continues, it builds the baby's body and the Nerve System. The infant is not formed of the mother's blood as science teaches. Creation never makes New Bodies of used material.

Here we face the great secret of Life! The Astral Rays that build the baby pierce the earth's Aura as the Silver Cord mentioned in the Bible, converge at the Fonticulus Frontalis in the human skull, called the Door opened in Heaven in the Bible (Rev. 4:1), and condense, as vapor condenses to form water and ice, producing the Spinal Cord and Nerve System, thru which Astral Light flows as an electric current being the mysterious Nerve Force of medical art, and produces the psychosomatic qualities of Vitality, Consciousness, Mind and Intelligence. Try to find that one in the great medical tomes of the haughty physicians.

And here's another one for medical art: In 1953 two Canadian doctors demonstrated by test that growing beets changed Astral Light into fiberous cellulose in ten seconds.

And here's still another one for medical art: During World War II, two doctors, working on radar equipment, made a killing discovery that did not leak out until the war closed. In ten seconds a man, standing in the invisible rays of a radar transmitter, felt uncomfortable heat sensations in his body. In less than a munute the instnsity of the heat made him move out of range. Within 15 days he died. The surface of his body showed no marks; but an examination of the interior showed that "his insides were cooked," said the doctors. "A hole as big as a silver dollar was burnt in his small bowel.

All this is regarded now as a great discovery. We are just recovering some lost Wisdom. All this was known to the Atlantean Masters twenty thousand years ago, who used the Death Ray to destroy their enemies.

The Death Ray is the Killing Aspect of Astral Light. The Life Ray is the Silver Cord aspect of Astral Light. All phases of Astral Light are electrican in their nature and have their good and evil qualities.

Living bodies are endowed with the power of movement by Astral Light flowing thru them as an electric current. The same current produces movement in trucks. But trucks do not possess the psychosomatic states of Man called Consciousness, Mind and Intelligence. The difference is not in the nature of the motivating power, but in the nature of the mechanism.

A live wire is one charged with Fire called Electricity. When the charge is absent the wire is called "dead." But there is no apparent change in the wire itself.

So it is with the human body. Extract the Living Fire from it and it is as dead as a log. This perfect analogy between a living body and a live wire should be kept in mind, as it leads to surprising results.

The Masters were right in their opinion when they used Fire as a symbol of Life. Now watch and see how simple we find the Creator for whom scientists have searched in vain for ages. How can we find Him when we know not what He is?

The Bible says He dwells in the human body, and there is where we shall find Him. The big question is whether we can persuade the reader to believe what the Bible says.

A pin cannot be pressed against the body anywhere without touching a Nerve. Nerves are "physical wires" that are charged,during life, without what science calls Nerve Force and its basic origin.

Physicians are taught that Life is just a series of chemical changes occurring in the cells of the body. They must accept what their schools teach "or else." If they question what they are taught, their license as a physician is revoked on a charge of "unethical conduct."

Systematic standardization controls our civilization and must be preserved. Doctors and pastors must stay in line or get out. That means the rejection of all progress that fails to fit in the framework of this standardization. In that circle our leaders must travel and stay.

Man would be amazed if he could see his Nerve System in its entirety. It would present in his sight the same size and shape of his body. The Nerves are interlaced, interwoven and interblended so completely and perfectly with the flesh and bone, that, in our sight, the Temple of the Creator and the human body would appear as one.

This Nerve System is the Temple of the Spiritual Fire as stated in the Bible (1 Cor. 3:16). This is the terrible Lord mentioned in the Bible (Ps. 47:2). This was the El Shaddai of the Hebrews, which means "terrible powers," "that which treats with violence," etc. Ages before the Hebrews, the Hindus called the Lord Jaggernath--"ruthless power."

This is the terrific system of Flashing Fire that science discovered when it got too close to the Creator in splitting the atom. This is the Fire in which we do actually live, and move, and have our being, as the Bible says, (Acts 17:28).

The Creator is absolutely Omnipresent and appears in every created object, attaining His highest level of manifestation in the formation called Man.

When we gaze in a mirror, we see only the physical frame. That is another illusion. For we are really looking at the form of Flashing Fire which men call God but cannot find because they know not for what to look.

-141-

We have uncovered the mysterious Unknowable Reality of Dr.
Carrel and Herbert Spencer, and answered that serious question of
the late Dr. Millikan, who did not know why he was alive rather than
read (Collier's, Oct. 25, 1925).

And so, what is Man? Grahame W. Barratt, writing in Psychic
Observer under the title, Spiritual Truth in Pyramid Egypt, said:--

"In all the world there is only one story, and that is the story
of Man. He rises from and melts back again into the background
Principle of his own true universal Self."

We are presenting that story of Man as related in the Bible and
by the Masters of the Ancient Wisdom--Man created in the image and
likeness of God. If we refuse to believe the story, we must continue
to wander in darkness, for our scientists can tell us practically
nothing about Man, frankly admitting that, to them, Man is an Unknowable Reality and an unsolvable riddle.

In the words of Dr. Alexis Carrel, one of the truly great scientists of this century, here is what science admits:--

"The science of Man is the most difficult of all sciences (p.10).
Men of science know not where they are going. They are guided by
accident and chance (p. 23). Those (scientists) who investigate the
phenomena of Life are as if lost in an inextricable jungle, in the
midst of a magic forest, whose countless trees unceasingly change
their place and their shape (p. 1). Man is composed of a procession
of phantoms, in the midst of which strides an unknowable reality (p.4).
The functions of the most complex organs of the body still remain
unknown (p. 34). Our intelligence can no more realize the immensity
of the brain than the extent of the sidereal universe (p. 95). We
know not the relations between consciousness and the nervous processes (p. 97). Immense regions of our inner world (of our body) are
still unknown (p. 4). An endocrinologist, a psychoanalyst, a biological chemist are all equally ignorant of Man. Most of the questions
put to themselves by those (scientists) who study human beings remain
unanswered. In fact, our ignorance (of man) is profound (p. 4). It
is impossible, for the present, to grasp the body's constitution. We
must, then, be content with the scientific observation of our organic
and mental activities, and , with no other guide, march forward unto
the unknown" (p. 109) (Man The Unknown).

These frank statements of a great scientist fall far short of
agreeing with the wild propaganda appearing in the press and the big
periodicals that constantly laud the March of Science. The bald facts
show that it is the March of Ignorance.

-142-

And Carrel presents the serious type of blasting ignorance that is instilled into the tender minds of children by the vigorous brainwashing processes of the schools dominated by this very same science.

When these children attend church and Sunday-school, they are exposed to another type of brainwashing that leaves them bewildered and confused.

The spot in the skull where the Silver Cord penetrates the Golden Bowl (head) is called the Fonticulus Frontalis, as we have said. To this important fontanel the medical books pay no special attention. If it has a particular purpose, the medical books fail to notice it. Why consume time and money in any research that presents no possibilities in the form of dimes and dollars?

In man's skull there are seven fontanels. This one, much the largest, is the soft spot in the top of a baby's head where the bones do not close immediately. Sometimes they never close at this point, but usually the sutures unite between the second and fifth years.

This knowledge concerning the human body, so mysterious now and practically unknown to the great scientists, was common knowledge in the ancient world, and was contained in the scrolls that were destroyed when the ancient libraries were burned to destroy the Ancient Wisdom.

This knowledge still appears in the ancient scrolls of India, where they were beyond the reach of the destructive hand of the Roman Despots. In them the Fonticulus Frontalis is called the Brahamarandhra, the Aperture of Brahma, the Throne of Shiva, the Seat of the Nibodhika Fire.

Penetrating the skull as a radar beam, at the Door Opened in Heaven, the Silver Cord, composed of the same Astral Light that creates the Rainbow in its seven colors, enters the brain as an invisible ray, gradually condensing, growing visible in the brain as Nerves, which converge at the medulla oblongata portion of the brain, and there form the Spinal Cord, as we have said.

The Creator, flowing thru the brain and nerves as an electrical current, builds, sustains and control the entire body and its functions, presenting the peculiar qualities of Vitality, Consciousness, Mind and Intelligence, which are such a mystery to science, to medical art, and to the doctors, with the one exception of the leading chiropractors.

This Ancient Wisdom was known to the biblical makers, and was so well hidden by them, that the Silver Cord is mentioned but once in the Bible, and then in terms that tell nothing to the exoteric and the uninitiated.

This is the secret reason why the monks of all nations, unto this day, keep their hair shaved over the Fonticulus Frontalis, to facilitate, as they seem to think, the freer passage of the Silver Cord thru the Door Opened in Heaven.

It is well to incorporate here an account of an actual event that occurred, which reveals some of the mystery of the Ego and the Silver Cord.

In Fate Magazine of October, 1953, Margaret Linden told an interesting story of her passing out of her physical body thru the Door Opened in Heaven and returning to it again, as one does in dreams. She was ill and rushed to a hospital for surgery. A couple hours after the operation she related this amazing experience:

"I found myself back in bed and was reviving from the effect of the anaesthetic, and could hear myself crying, 'Don't send me back!'

"I remember trying to move my inert body, and of being restrained by the doctor, who held both of my hands, I could hear him speaking quietly, insistently, striving to impress upon my subconscious that it must hold fast to the remembrance of why I was begging 'not to be sent back.'

"When I returned to full consciousness the next day, the doctor was there, and asked, 'Do you remember?' I did and I do now. At some time during the operation, I--my Ego--left my body. I was flying, and I knew it was no dream. For I had died; I knew it, and I welcomed it.

"It was far more wonderful than any dream. I was no longer confined in my body. I was lighter than a feather; I had no weight, no substance at all. I was just an essence, a vital spark, equipped with thoughts, feelings, senses and consciousness. The one sensation above all others was that of great joy.

"I could hear magnificent music, and it seemed that I was the center of it (Music of the Spheres). And as I was savoring this ecstasy in its entirety, a voice, that seemed to come from me, commanded: 'You must go back; you must go back.' And I had a feeling that I was being pushed downward. I cried, I implored, but again came that command: 'You must go back.'

"And down I came, faster and faster, until, with a crash, I felt myself being pushed into what seemed to be a box of lead, which my Ego knew was my body.

"After telling the doctor this story, he said that near the end of the operation, I had no pulse, no breath, no heart beat. I was apparently dead. He had quickly inserted his fingers thru the incision in my body, and massaged my heart, hoping to start is action. He succeeded--and I was alive again in my body. I did not die, but my body had died."

This is a description by one who returned to the body after going over the brink, as in the case of the Neophyte when initiated in the Ancient Mysteries. The Silver Cord did not break, and the Ego returned to the body.

This describes that terrifying process of dying, governed by law just as in the case of being born. It's all over, says the Bible, "in the twinkling of an eye" (Cor. 15:52). Practically the same story is told by all who go thru that experience.

Knowledge of this creative process was one of the secrets of initiation in the Ancient Mysteries. The Neophyte was hypnotized, his Ego left his body, gazed down at it, and then returned. He thus had the Keys of Life and Death as the Bible says (Rev. 1:18).

Reversing the order of the Nerve System, when the Nerves return from the body to the brain as the Spinal Cord, they don't end in the brain as science teaches. They change from fibrous sinews to bluish-white rays, converging at the Sahasrara Chakra as the Hindus called it, the Fonticulus Frontalis as we call it, and the Door Opened in Heaven as the Bible calls it.

In the ancient Sanscrit, this port of entry of the Silver Cord into the brain was called Brahma-Randhra, and translated "hole". The term could be better translated "cavity." The Hindus called it the "Gateway of the Soul," the point of ingress and egress of the Living Fire, the Eternal Ego.

And this is the explanation of the secret of Jacob's Ladder, set up on earth (Spinal Cord in the body), and the top (Silver Cord) reaching up to heaven (Astral World), the Abode of Shiva as the Hindus called it, with angels ascending and descending.

The Angels, of course, represent the Ego entering the human body and leaving it, and signifying the route by which Man returns to the Astral World. Pol tells the story in the Bible in these words:

-145-

Behold, I show you a mystery: We shall not sleep (in death), but we shall be CHANGED, in a moment, in the twinkling of an eye, at the last trump. For the trumpet (of Gabriel) shall sound (as symbolized in Card 20 of the Ancient Tarot), and the Ego, regarded as dead while confined in the body, shall be raised incorruptible, as indicated in said Card 20, and we shall be changed (from mortality to immortality).

Now this event is actually that Resurrection (of the Ego) taught by the Masters, and never meant the resurrection of the body, which Pol referred to when he said "that flesh and blood cannot inherit the kingdom of God; neither doth corruption (the body) inherit incorruption" (1 Cor. 15:50).

And the great Master Pol knew by experience the cold facts which he preached; for he was an Initiate of the Ancient Mysteries, had been hypnotized, left his body, and gazed down at it, as Margaret Linden and thousands of others have done.

Pol continued: For this corruptible (body) must put on incorruption, and this mortal (body) must put on immortality. So when this corruptible shall have put on incorruption, and this mortal shall have put on immortality (which occurs when the Ego leaves the corruptible body), then shall be brought to pass the saying that is written (in Isa. 25:8), Death is swallowed up in victory. O death, where is thy sting?O Grave, where is thy victory?-- (1 Cor. 5:51-55).

For we know that if our earthy house (body) were dissolved, we have a building of God (Ego), and house not made with hands, eternal in the heavens (2 Cor. 5:1).

Here Pol refers to the two bodies, the Celestial and the Terrestrial; and we must not disregard the fact that the Celestial Body, meaning the Ego, he definitely said was "the Lord from Heaven." We have here clearly presented the exact meaning of all these statements of Pol (1 Cor. 15:40-47).

There is another statement in the Bible that refers to the Ego, that Lord from Heaven, saying the Ego is "dead" while inhabiting the body, and alive when liberated from the body in the creative process called Death. It says:

I am he (the Ego) that liveth, and was dead (while confined in the body); and behold, (I was not dead for) I am alive for evermore (being liberated from the body by its death), and I have the Keys of Life and Death (Rev. 1:18).

And this same Pol, in allegory, refers to himself when he was initiated in the Ancient Mysteries, and states that after his initia-

-146-

tion he was clad in a garment dyed red, as a mark of distinction, and he was given a new name, being called the Son of Light (Rev. 19:13).

The phraseology is purposely twisted in the Bible to conceal the facts from the exoteric and the profane, a course pursued all thru the book.

Such is the mystery of Man, a being that science has never been able to classify nor describe. Carrel said that he "is made up of a procession of phantoms, in the midst of which (there) strides an unknowable reality," and the Bible tells us that this Unknowable Reality is the Spirit of God that dwells in the human body (1 Cor. 3:16; 15:47).

Therefore, according to the Bible, "the Lord from Heaven" appears upon the earth in the human form called Man, created in the image and likeness of the Creator, which means that Man is a Reflection of the Creator as symbolized by the Masters in their Interlaced Triangle, and as stated in the Bible, which statements are considered symbolical by those who do not understand the nature of Life and the constitution of Man. But now we see that these are really a few of the passages in the Bible that can be accepted fundamentally and literally.

In the marvelous Nerve System there flows the Creator as a stream of Astral Light, called Electricity and Nerve Force, and discovered by accident in 1895 by Palmer. And what do the great physicians know about this Nerve System, its purpose and function? Let them speak and tell us:

The Associated Press, reporting a speech delivered June 19,1961, at Atlantic City by Dr. Harold G. Wolff, President of the American Neurological Association, quoted this great Neurologist as stating:

"Overwhelming evidence has been gathered during thirty years of study to show that nearly all disease involves the nervous system These important findings suggest that more emphasis should be placed in the future on psychosomatic medicine."

Think of spending that much time and money researching this subject when the great medical experts, had they stooped that low, could have secured the same dope and data from any competent chiropractor long before they started their studies.

After the people peruse the wild propaganda of miracle medicine and wonder drugs that flows so constantly from medical circles, it is difficult to persuade them to believe that such gross ignorance of body function can prevail in medical art. It is not surprising that young and vigorous patients die so frequently under orthodox medical care.

The whole Nerve System is not only involved in all of the body's processes, whether regular physiology or irregular pathology, but that System filled with the Living Fire flowing from the Astral World is directly responsible for the movement of every cell, of every muscle, every wink of the eye, every smile and scowl, every word man speaks, every thought he thinks, every beat of his heart, every breath he draws, the flowing of his blood, the digestion of his food, the elimination of the body's filth, and for those strange qualities of the body that are such a mystery to science, viz., Vitality, Consciousness, Mind and Intelligence.

Knowing so little about the Nerve System, its purpose and function, how can these great physicians understand the nature and the source of the quaternary qualities that make Man a Living Soul.

And the bald facts of Life, of Man, and of Creation, when known and understood, are much more amazing than the wildest fiction invented by puny man, the copyist.

The greatest mysteries of the Universe are the greatest simplicities when properly presented and correctly comprehended. What is more simple than a tree growing from an apple seed, and yet the greatest scientist cannot analyze the process.

The Life Link

The Silver Cord, extending from the Astral World and linking the Microcosm to the Macrocosm, the Created to the Creator, the body of flesh to the living Spirit, may be compared to the umbilical cord that links the unborn baby to its mother.

The Silver Cord may be regarded as analogous to a radar-beam that extends for miles into space, and along which air-planes and missiles may be guided accurately by puny man, the copyist.

Doctors report many instances where patients, undergoing surgery leave the body as Margaret Linden did during her operation, and look down at the unconscious shell, as the Initiates used to do in the Ancient Mysteries.

In such instances, the Living Spirit is evulsed from the physical prison, yet remains united to it by the Silver Cord, by which the Spirit of God can return and reactivate the shell, if the cord remains intact.

The Silver Cord, constituted of Astral Light, is capable of infinite extension. In sleep we may, as in dreams, leave the body
thru the Door In Heaven and fly miles away in an instant. The body
remains "alive" and we return to it as long as the Silver Cord remains unbroken. But when it breaks, somatic death results.

The time is sure to come when the leading chiropractors will
learn more about the real nature of the Nerve System, and then chiropractic colleges will teach that the Silver Cord of the Macrocosm
and the Spinal Cord of the Microcosm are actually one, being a con-
tinuation of each other, the materialized portion being in the
material body, and the astral portion extending into the Astral World.

At the base end of the spinal portion of the Cord in the material body is the creative power of the Microcosm, and in the upper
portion of the Cord, in the Astral World, is the creative power of
the Macrocosm.

This explains the mystery of Jacob's Ladder. The Fiery Creator
is symbolized as an angel descending on the ladder, and that process is called Birth. In due time, the angel leaves the body thru
the Door In Heaven and ascends the Ladder. That process is called
Death, the Born Again doctrine of the Bible, and understood by the
Masters who said, "Better is the day of thy Death than the day of
thy Birth" (Eccl. 7:1; John 3:3, 5, 7).

We have reversed the situation, rejoicing at the birth of the
baby and lamenting at the death of the body.

Expiration

A certain man lay on his death-bed. He was noted for the trust-
ing faith in his mind, was a so-called Free Thinker, and many were
the nights that he had sat, discussing with friends, the great ques-
tion--What comes after Death? "If a man die, shall he live again?"
--Job 14:14.

Now, in his dying moments, he was only seconds away from the
answer. Suddenly his eyes opened widely. His gaze seemed to pierce
the ceiling. A happy smile appeared on his face. As the last
breath was leaving his body, he whispered: "Ah, at last, the Great
Secret."

What was the Great Secret which he witnessed as he slipped out
of his body thru the Door Opened in Heaven?

Margaret Linden told that story, and the same story is told by many others who have been at the brink of transition, but failed to pass over.

First, there is a sensation of surprising levity of the body. Before the person is willing to let nurse or doctor know that strange things are occurring in his mind, he begins to sense that he is not lying so heavily. At first he thinks it's his imagination. Then he begins to sense a pleasant warmth, and to feel that he could rise from the bed and nothing could stop him.

The room begins to change. The walls begin to appear farther away. This sensation is not due to fading sight, as he still recognizes those present. That is the secret of the Fourth Dimension, when the mind begins to contact a new world, in which both space and time are absent. The mind begins to extend beyond the limits of space and time and grow omnipotent. This indicates the fading of physical consciousness and the dawning of Cosmic Consciousness.

Then the voices of those present begin to fade, until it seems they are at the far end of a long hall. This indicates the fading out of physical impressions and the dawning of metaphysical sensations.

Eventually, the unconscious person sees nothing but his own body on the bed. Not with his physical eyes, for his physical sight has been succeeded by metaphysical sight. He is now entering the Astral World, and seems to be several feet above his bed, gazing down at the body.

This scene is portrayed on certain Egyptian monuments, showing Osiris lying on his bier, with the Ego in the form of a hawk hovering over the body. Beneath the bier are most of the crowns of Osiris, and beside it stands Isis.

Between him and his body a dim haze appears. This is the Silver Cord in which is the Ego, the Spirit of God, the Real Man, and he looks with Astral Sight now, as one looks thru a fine veil over one's face.

Dr. Arthur A. Beale of London wrote some interesting observations on the Silver Cord that fit in here. He said:--

"There have been many cases, even to the knowledge of myself, where patients have left their bodies and were able to look down on the unconscious shell from above.

"In such cases the complete entity (Ego) is separated or evulsed from the physical body, and yet remains anchored to it by a tenuous cord of astral substance,by means of which the entity is able to return and reactivate the shell, provided the cord is not broken.

"Should the cord, for any reason, snap or sever, then such person would be reported as "dead", and his body would be dead. (What keeps the cord from breaking at this moment? The condition of the body. The cord does not break as long as the body remains fit for the in-dwelling of the Spirit of God.)

"This is not imagery, for, apart from the stated experience of the person himself, were a trained occultist, or even a clairvoyant, present at the time of the phenomena, he could see and describe the comatose physical body and the divorced or separated entity, hovering over it, joined by the Silver Cord like an umbilical cord of the new-born baby."

This is the mysterious process of the Ego's leaving the body in death, as described by those who have recovered from death-like con-ditions. It is similar to struggling thru a dark, narrow tunnel (Door In Heaven) out into a big, brightly lighted place. The typical experience of the infant during and immediately after being born of the mother.

Those who return state that in the dying process, the Mind becomes clearer than ever before, and the head becomes intensely brilliant, like a bright, Golden Bowl. And the Silver Cord grows stronger at this moment, to protect the Ego contained it, as it flows out of the Fonticulus Frontalis like a rapidly moving fluorescent light, im-perceptibly extracting the body's vitality on the order of a suction pump.

Thus, the Fiery Creator leaves the body thru the Door Opened in Heaven as a beam of Astral Light that may be seen by a true clair-voyant.

In the Orient, diagrams portraying this remarkable process are comparatively common. These diagrams show a beam of Golden Light rising from the Gate of Brahma in the crown of the head.

When the Silver Cord breaks, the Ego is entirely released from its earthy prison, and, for Man, that is a moment of marked import. It cannot be too strongly urged upon relatives that it is a crime against the departing Ego to give expression of loud lamentations at this time. For the Ego is engaged in a great process, and much of the value of the earthy life-experience of the Ego depends upon the attention now given to that matter. Loud lamentations of those pre-sent seriously disturb that attention.

-151-

And furthermore, it is a crime against the dying person to give
stimulants to force the departing Ego back into the body, thus giv-
ing a great shock to a dying person. It is peaceful to leave the
body in the dying-process, but torturous to be forced back into it
by stimulants, to cause more suffering to the body.

Relatives make a big mistake under the impression that they are
aiding the dying by trying to keep the body alive. In that foolish
way many are kept dying for hours, thus prolonging the suffering of
the body.

Also, the body should not be cremated nor embalmed until at least
three days after death. For the Ego is still attached to the body
by a fine cord, which does not part until the panorama of the earthy
experience of the Ego, in that incarnation, has been reviewed.

That is the esoteric meaning of the three days and three nights
in the heart of the earth (Mat. 12:40). The meaning of the Last
Judgment is the review of the earthy experience of the Ego.

Further reference to the three-day-period appears in the Bible
where it is said, "After two days he will revive us; and in the
third day he will raise us up, and we shall live (forever) in his
sight" (Hosea 6:2).

The Empty Sarcophagus

In the ancient Symbolism, an Empty Sarcophagus usually signified
the flight of the Ego from its physical prison.

This closing event in man's earthy life is symbolized in Card
20 of the Ancient Tarot, titled the Last Judgment. It pictures the
Angel Gabriel who presides over all that is powerful. From his aura
shafts of Astral Light shoot down to the earth, indicating the human
nature of the sign. He blows a trumpet, as mentioned in the Bible
(1 Cor. 15:52), and from its bell there radiate 7 lines, indicating
the 7 incarnations the Ego must experience to become an Individualized Entity.

On a banner attached to the trumpet is the Solar Cross, signify-
ing the four fixed signs of the Zodiakos, Aries, Cancer, Libra and
Capricorn, which indicate the Sacred Four Elements, Fire, Air, and
Earth.

Below the Angel is a Sarcophagus, representing the tomb in which
the Ego is buried during its earthy existence, and from which there

now emerge the figures of a man, a woman and a child, wonder, adoration and ecstasy being expressed by their attitudes.

This card symbolizes the principal part of the ceremony of the Ancient Mysteries that marked the completion of the Initiation of the Candidate, after which, as stated in the Bible, he was clad in a vesture dyed red as a mark of distinction, and he was called The Son of Light (Rev. 19:13).

In the King's Chamber of the Great Pyramid of Gizeh the modern investigators were surprised and mystified to discover an empty, lidless Sarcophagus. The meaning of it has never been satisfactorily explained. That was the Stone Coffer in which was placed the Candidate, who was then in a deep hypnotic trance, and was guarded by two who were Adepts of high degree. At the end of the third day, a Herald appeared and announced the "Victory over Death" (Isaiah 25:8), and awakened the Candidate from his hypnotic trance.

The child, emerging from the tomb in Card 20, represents such Candidate, who was symbolized as a child because he had just been reborn. For he who had passed thru the last crucial test was called the Twice Born, mentioned in the Bible as Born Again (John 3:3,5,7).

The real tomb of the Ego on the earth plane is the physical body, in which the Masters said it was "cabined, cribbed and confined" so that it may develop Individualization, a state that can be created in no other way, and the principal reason why the physical body is created.

Sir Oliver Lodge said, "The Soul may return to the central store, but not without indentity." And that indentity can be acquired only by passing thru the creative process of Seven Incarnations on the earth plane, which knowledge appears in the Bible in this statement:

"And there are seven kings (incarnations); five (incarnations) are fallen and one (incarnation) is (present), and the other (incarnation) is not yet come; and when he (the seventh incarnation) cometh, he must continue for a short space" (of one life-span) (Rev. 17:10).

After the Ego has developed Individualization under the Law of Septennation, it has no more need to return to the earth, and passes forward to a state of Higher Consciousness beyond the jurisdiction of the physical plain, and in which the latter plain plays no further part.

The Inner Secrets of Initiation in the Ancient Mysteries were never placed on paper, and were never revealed to the profane and impious. For no Sacred Doctrine can long remain underfiled unless

-153-

protected from those not found qualified by appropriate test to receive the same. That is another reason why the esoteric character of the Ancient Wisdom was always protected by the most powerful sanctions.

An Oath of secrecy was administered in the most solemn form to the Initiate, as is still the case in Freemasonry, and to violate it was considered a sacrilegious crime, the prescribed punishment for which was immediate death.

Accordingly, the ancient authors were extremely reluctant to approach the subject, and they shruck from divulging or discussing any explanation of a symbol that had been interpreted to them in the Ritual of Initiation. That is the principal reason why the true interpretation of the Ancient Symbols does not appear in the Bible and never appeared in any of the ancient scriptures.

Horace said, "I would forbid that man who would divulge the sacred rites of mysterious Ceres from being under the same roof with me, of from setting sail with me in the same precarious bark."

Only by such confinement of the Ancient Wisdom, guarded by the most rigid rites, could the Masters expect to preserve it from the superstitions, innovations and corruptions of the world at large. For it is impossible to make satisfactory or serious impressions upon the mind of a fool with any knowledge, regardless of its greatness.

1961 The world wants to know who, what, and where is the Creator. Ages of searching by great men have failed to find Him. If there is a Creator, it should be possible to locate Him. If there is none, then there is no answer to the question, What Power Creates and Regulates the World and everything in it? All questions have answers. This one has an answer, and Hotema was determined not to stop digging till he found it. Where did he find it? Right in the Bible, but stated in terms so simple that no one had noticed it.